THE BOOK OF THE LINKS

SUTTON, COLT, DARWIN

ISBN: 1732113777
ISBN-13: 978-1732113770

First Published, 1912 by W.H. Smith & Son,

Contents

SUNT LACRYMAE RERUM

Porter (to Golfer, who is immensely proud of his set of clubs): "Where will you 'ave your 'ockey bats, sir?"

Illustrations

Preface

The title of this volume is somewhat bold, but I venture to hope that the reader who possesses sufficient patience to master the contents will not deem it unreasonable.

Though it is a worn-out adage that "of the making of many books there is no end," it is nevertheless a fact that matters appertaining to the golf course have not been over-written to the extent of some forms of sport, while the game is so many-sided as to permit of an almost infinite variety of treatment.

In producing this volume it has been my aim to provide in the first instance a compendium of information, of a more complete character than has before been compressed into a single volume, on all the points upon which golf secretaries, green committees, and greenkeepers desire instruction. If the subjects treated appear to cover a rather extensive field, it must be remembered that the secretary and committee of a golf club are practically in the position of managers of a small estate, so that any point connected with estate management will necessarily be of value to them.

But it is hoped that there is also much in the book to interest, and possibly to amuse, the ordinary golfer—and who is not a golfer at the present day?—while it may help to show him how much is involved in the construction and upkeep of his favourite course.

The writers who have collaborated with me, and whose names appear at the head of their articles, are universally recognised to be leading authorities on the subjects with which they deal; and if this work in any way fulfils the purpose already referred to, I shall be more than recompensed for the time and labour expended on its production.

I may add that, with a view to facilitate reference to any subject of special interest to the reader, a complete index will be found at the end of the book.

MARTIN H. F. SUTTON

Reading, 1912

Chapter I

The Construction of New Courses

By H. S. Colt

Every golfer is inclined to have very decided views upon the merits of a course or the merits of a hole. Sometimes it may be that his exceptional abilities for playing a particular stroke assist him materially in forming his opinion, and possibly—although no doubt one may be wrong in this suggestion—his want of skill urges him to decide with no uncertainty that a particular hole is not golf at all, and that a particular bunker is the creation of a madman or of an ill-natured idiot.

Although these are extreme cases and need no attention from the so-called golf architect, still some healthy criticism of his efforts, in spite of being somewhat distasteful at times, will do him no harm, and will very likely prove a help.

It does not seem to follow that because a man is a good player he is a good judge of a course. On a recent occasion a hole towards the end of the round, which was a particularly dull example of the drive and pitch description, had been altered so as to require a carefully "placed" tee shot and then a long iron shot to reach the green, which bristled with difficulties. A friend of mine, who was a first-class golfer, had been playing with two friends who were not his equals in skill. On finishing his round he came up to me and remarked that it seemed a pity to spoil the course completely. I inquired in what way we had erred, and his reply was: "Why, the 17th hole is entirely spoilt. Before it was altered it did require a pitch, but now any silly fool can get a four." I pondered over the remark, but the subsequent pecuniary transactions made the reason slightly plainer.

On the other hand, there are many long-handicap players who seem to possess a large amount of sympathy for the first-class player, and, if not able themselves to bring off shots requiring exceptional skill, will appreciate thoroughly the way in which they can be played. Moreover, it is not by any means impossible to construct a course which will give pleasure and amusement to all classes of players. A few years back one often heard it stated that a course, to be a good test of golf, should be laid out for the scratch player, and there were many instances of quite impossible shots being provided for the long-handicap man, without any opportunity of playing for safety. On one championship course a carry used to be provided for certain competitions which in the teeth of a strong wind was quite impossible, and I have seen ex-champions playing meekly into the middle of the bunker with an iron club so as to avoid being under the face, as there was no possibility of safety. Fancy always having to do this! Yet the short driver has still many enemies of this description, so the reverse is only natural; and there are instances of retaliation, the short player preparing pitfalls for the best efforts of the long hitter, so that when he has hit the ball in the centre of the club, straight in the desired line, he may find it trapped, and thus be compelled to yield up the hole to his short-slicing opponent.

In this connection it may be well to bear in mind that golf is primarily a pastime and not a penance, and that the player should have a chance of extracting from a game the maximum amount of pleasure with the minimum amount of discomfort as punishment for his evil ways. He will not obtain this pleasure unless you provide plenty of difficulties; but surely there is no need for vindictiveness. And just think how pleasant it is to hop over a bunker at times, and occasionally hit a wild shot and have a chance of recovery! There is opportunity for much-needed mercy even to erratic golfers.

Seaside Courses

The nature of the soil is, no doubt, of great importance, but frequently there is no choice. The rolling sand dunes of the seashore cannot be always ready at hand for our course. It has only three or four times fallen to my lot to help in the construction of a course under these ideal conditions, and very pleasant work it was. There are some common difficulties in dealing with ground of this description. It often lies in a narrow strip by the shore, and the clubhouse is erected at one end of the selected site. In many cases force of circumstances insists upon this, but in others it can be avoided, and if the house be pitched more in the centre of the land the wind will be split up between the two nine holes and two starting-points will also be provided.

Wind—Everyone knows how pleasant it is, after striving against a strong wind and hitting harder and harder at each hole with less and less result, to turn one's back upon the gale for a hole or two and play gigantic shots down wind. After doing this we are refreshed, and feel in a mood to battle with the "brute" who tries to destroy our best efforts.

Hummocks—The sandy hummocks common to all of the best of the seaside courses, whilst being one of their finest features, also present some difficulty. On a new course it is often a hard matter to get this ground into good playing order, the covering of turf is so easily broken, especially on a downward slope in dry weather. When these hummocks are covered with good, sound turf they make excellent features and give difficult stances and lies; but at the start of a new course they are liable to be terrible traps. The expense of covering a large tract of this ground with turf must be very considerable, and quite beyond the means of most clubs, and so we often find that the "spirit-level" has been applied and some of the best features of the course flattened out, and a beautiful natural piece of golfing ground reduced to the level of a flat field. With a little patience these hummocks may be made "sound" by light and frequent dressings of rich sandy soil in which suitable seed has been mixed. A dressing composed of heavy soil will almost certainly prove a failure, and the seed mixture should correspond as nearly as possible to the varieties of grasses which exist in the natural turf.

On some sites a certain amount of judicious levelling will be needed, as otherwise the goat of Andrew Kirkaldy's story will be a more suitable inhabitant for the links than the perspiring golfer; but on the margins of the course there can hardly be too many sand dunes. As a guide on this point, the old course at St. Andrews seems to me to be a perfect example.

For bunkering work it is impossible to have better materials than these sandy hummocks, as, if the faces are just torn out, we obtain perfectly natural-looking hazards, thoroughly in keeping with the surroundings of the links. Yet how often do we see horrible symmetrical-looking pits, with faces smoothed out to the same angle, and the pleasant surroundings spoilt thereby! And very likely some old railway sleepers are used to prevent the sides of the hazards ever looking natural. What can be more incongruous in a sand bunker on a seaside course? They are no doubt useful laid lengthwise on the ground to form a narrow pathway; but, for preventing the sand from blowing, bent grasses, such as *Ammophila arundinacea* and *Elymus arenarius*, will do the work efficiently and look natural, and, to keep the sides from falling in, nothing is better than turf laid so as to form a rough, uneven face. But the sides of the bunkers can be allowed to become rugged and irregular in appearance, and not scraped with a spade, as if an asparagus bed were being constructed. The first time that I played over the Prince's Course at Sandwich one of the many delightful features that appealed to me was that the faces of the bunkers were invariably irregular in appearance, and I believe that these bunkers were, so to speak, "dragged out" with forks or other implements, and spades were not used at all for the work.

Water—The water supply is another difficulty common to seaside courses, and this has driven many to select hollows for the putting greens and not plateaux. Ground of the latter description is liable to become parched in the summer, when the golfing season is at its height. On many inland links the summer months are generally the slackest; if the greens are not quite perfect then, it does not matter so much as in the spring and autumn. At one time I thought that water was not a necessity, but recent experience has made me alter my opinion, unless the rainfall for the district is well above the average. With an artificial supply of water many extra opportunities are given to the designer of a golf course. He need not consider whether a certain acceptable site for a putting green is likely to dry up too quickly if it is on a slope facing the south or lies on a plateau. A plentiful supply of water from a reliable source, with a good pressure, so that three or four greens can be watered at the same time, will help largely towards the success of a club, as there can be then very little excuse for bad putting greens.

The Old Course, St. Andrews

Bunker at the 11th, Sunningdale

Sometimes artesian wells are sunk at convenient places, and portable oil engines brought into operation to work the pumps. But there is often a risk of the supply of water becoming brackish, and although a slight amount of salt therein will not matter, and may even do some good, if it be present beyond a certain percentage the result will be bad.

Treatment—The soil varies greatly on seaside courses, and not only on different courses, but on the same links. On some there is a good depth, and on others the merest sprinkling, and in such cases frequent dressings of light, rich soil must be applied. These, with the help of the horse roller, will improve the turf better than anything else. We must get a firm surface, and when the dressing has worked in to some extent the roller can be used. It is dangerous to apply a thick dressing of heavy soil, as it may cake on the surface and very likely kill the grass underneath. After the application of a dressing I always like to see the tips of the grass shoots above the soil, and the plants not completely smothered. But when enriching the soil it is quite possible to overdo it, and gradually change the character of the turf to such an extent that we have almost good fatting land for bullocks instead of a clean, close-growing turf suitable for the game of golf. As soon as an even, firm coat of turf is obtained we must stop enriching the soil and watch proceedings. If the course deteriorates, let us at once give it some help, but not until we see some slight sign of this coming about. In the dressing some good Peruvian guano can be added, and from my experience there is no better manure for this purpose; and in the case of all new courses add some seed to the dressing. There is sure to be a lot of moss and weeds present in the rough covering of the land, and constant slight renovations with seed are certain to give good results. The expense is very small, and I would use it not only in the early autumn and spring dressings, but also through the winter, as if mild weather intervenes the seed will germinate, and the loss of young plants will be but slight. I have recently had quite a success, although the seed was sown late in November; no doubt there was a risk, but we had to renovate the course after an abnormally dry summer, and the saving of time justified the risk.

It will be best to turf the very worst portions of the course, if it is possible to do so, and a little rich soil thereunder, especially on mounds, will do good; but it is often difficult to get the turf, and then we have to rely on seed.

In constructing a new course it is advisable to make a grass nursery, as a supply of turf is constantly needed for repairs and for new greens and teeing grounds. Four or five acres of good turf generally prove to be one of the club's most valuable assets. Good ground should be selected for the site, and if a little moist (not a swamp) so much the better, as the young plants will develop quicker.

All new courses want careful nursing, and this applies even more to new seaside courses than to others, and constant rolling, dressing, and seeding during the spring, autumn, and winter will work wonders in a comparatively short time. The construction of the teeing grounds and putting greens is dealt with in another chapter.

HEATHER COURSES

The heathland course has of late years come into special prominence. Walton Heath, Sunningdale, Woking, and Worplesdon are all instances of popular links of this description, and there are many others. As a class they particularly appeal to me, and, although it may seem almost heresy to say so, the best heather courses always appear to me to be quite as good from a golfing point of view as the majority of the seaside links. There are many who can see no merit in anything inland; but, on the other hand, there are many who can see but little merit in some of the much-vaunted seaside courses, and the admirers of the best inland links are an increasing body. We cannot have a St. Andrews or a Hoylake, but we can have something up to the standard of the majority of the seaside courses, although suffering from the disadvantages of being inland.

Expense—The construction of a course in a heather country is very costly, as the heather has to be ploughed up in the first place, the roots burnt, probably a large quantity of manure added, and grass seed sown over the whole of the playing area. You cannot get any good result under a year, and it generally means two years at least before the turf is really sound; and if the expense of a full-length course of this description works out at less than £4,000 or £5,000, it is cheap, unless there be special advantageous circumstances.

Drainage—In many of these courses there is a large amount of peat, and when the turf really begins to take root it seems to stand the drought well, owing to the decayed vegetation in the soil known as humus. But this very advantage may end in disaster unless care be taken to drain the subsoil. One green at Sunningdale had always been a mystery to me; it lay high, had plenty of soil for the roots of the grass, was always carefully nursed in bad weather, and yet never seemed to be entirely satisfactory. I remember a year or two ago purchasing some pigs from a farmer, who described the offspring of a certain sow, which he pointed out to me with pride, as really good "doers." It is a somewhat expressive term, and every greenkeeper will know that certain greens are good "doers" and others just the reverse, and this green was amongst the latter. My friend, Hugh McLean, our greenkeeper at Sunningdale, often had rather a puzzled look on his face when we came to it during our weekly inspection. We would examine the top with great care, and at times even crawl about on our hands and knees, much to the annoyance of the people waiting to play their approach shots. It never seemed to be bad enough to lift, and in the summer it was excellent. We cut a small hole or two in it, to see if the roots of the grass were healthy, and looked in the soil for grubs, and, in fact, took endless trouble. Eventually we hardened our hearts and stripped a big section, to the consternation of the members (Hugh and I are becoming accustomed to that), and on digging underneath we came to a bed of peat. It appears that when the course was constructed this soil was carted from a low-lying sour portion of the land and used for the green, and as it had never been broken up into small pieces and mixed with sharp, gritty materials, it had gradually consolidated and become sour. This was easily remedied, and I trust that the green will adopt a better course of life in future.

It is difficult to overdrain a golf course, and on these peaty courses it is most important to pay careful attention to the drainage. There are generally some boggy bits, which at first look hopeless for golf, and it may be necessary for the framework of the links to use them for play. If these places be carefully drained and some coke breeze be used, I have known them to become quite firm and sound. In drainage of this description it would be well to use 6-inch pipes for the main drains and 3-inch for the branch drains, which should be laid 2½ to 3 feet under the soil, and on the top of the pipes a 6-inch coating of gravel would help matters wonderfully. The expense would be considerable, amounting to a total cost of about 1*s.* per yard for the 6-inch mains and 9*d.* per yard for the 3-inch, but it would be worth it. In some districts the cost might conceivably be less, as labour is expensive with us and cartage and freight high.

Lime—There is another matter which is sometimes overlooked in connection with this class of course: it is the application of lime. Everyone who is a gardener knows how rhododendrons flourish amidst peaty surroundings, and at the same time how they dislike chalk. And greenkeepers know—or, at any rate, they ought to know—the necessity for lime being present in the soil if the turf is to be healthy. Some will remember the covering of the course at Sunningdale with a good dressing of lime soon after it was opened for play. Personally, I shall never forget it. Everyone that I met alluded to it; everybody's boots brought it vividly to my mind. The majority had discussed the merits of lime, or rather its demerits, with learned gardeners (probably of the jobbing type), and the adverse verdict was unanimous. The only friends left to me in the club were the three members of the Green Committee, and they were indeed staunch ones. However, in time the lime disappeared, and the result proved its efficacy. Where previously there was miserable dyspeptic-looking turf we had a good growth of healthy grass, and life became endurable once again. Now it is possible to obtain ground lime which can be spread by a machine of cunning device, so as to give no cause for grumbling, even to the most unfortunate player amongst your members. It is true the first result of lime is to encourage clover, but it is a recognised fact, I believe, amongst well-known authorities on agricultural chemistry that lime is a necessity for healthy grass, and if there is none in the soil, then it must be applied.

Porous Surface—Mention must be made of one more common difficulty with regard to this class of course—the necessity of obtaining and retaining a porous surface for the turf. This sort of soil is very liable to cake on the top, and if this happens it is quite impossible to get a healthy growth. Any sharp, gritty material, free from dangerous chemicals, worked into the surface will keep it porous. Worms will do this, but they are most obnoxious to golfers, and so we have to use artificial means to effect it. Charcoal is very useful, and also keeps the soil sweet; coke breeze, ground clinkers, and sharp sand are all good, and there are, no doubt, many other hard, gritty materials suitable for the purpose.

General Treatment—The first thing to do when starting to make a course in a country of this description is to cut down the heather close to the surface, rake it into heaps, and burn it. Then plough the land with the ploughshare set as deeply as possible, and cross-plough the site. Afterwards a subsoil plough can be used, as it is advisable to get as deep a cultivation as possible, and I should not now be satisfied with less than about 12 inches. Harrows can then be put on and the roots of the heather collected and burnt in slow fires, so that the ashes will be of use presently for the grass. It may be necessary to plough and harrow the land several times so as to get a good fine tilth. As soon as this has been obtained, a dressing of lime, containing a percentage of about 98 percent of carbonate of lime, can be given at the rate of about 1 ton to the acre; after this is well slaked and all the burning properties consumed, the manure can be spread on the surface. Rich horse manure, short and free from straw, should be obtained and used at the rate of from 15 to 20 tons to the acre—less in the case of good land, and even more in the case of very poor land. Let this be harrowed into the soil, and then the surface can be rolled either with a Cambridge roller or an ordinary double-cylinder roller, a dry day being chosen for the work.

It is better to let the land consolidate as much as possible before sowing the seed, and if the seedbed is prepared in this way a month or six weeks before sowing, so much the better. After ploughing has been finished and a fine tilth obtained it is almost impossible to have the land too firm, as the seed will grow much better in a solid bed than in loose soil. I have always noticed that the seed germinates better in the tracks of the wheels of a cart, which has passed over the land after sowing has taken place, than in the adjoining ground; one can see the marks of the wheels quite plainly by a dense growth of grass. If there is plenty of time (there generally is a rush to get the work done) it will give an opportunity to rid the site of weeds, which have grown in the meantime, before the seed is sown. A still

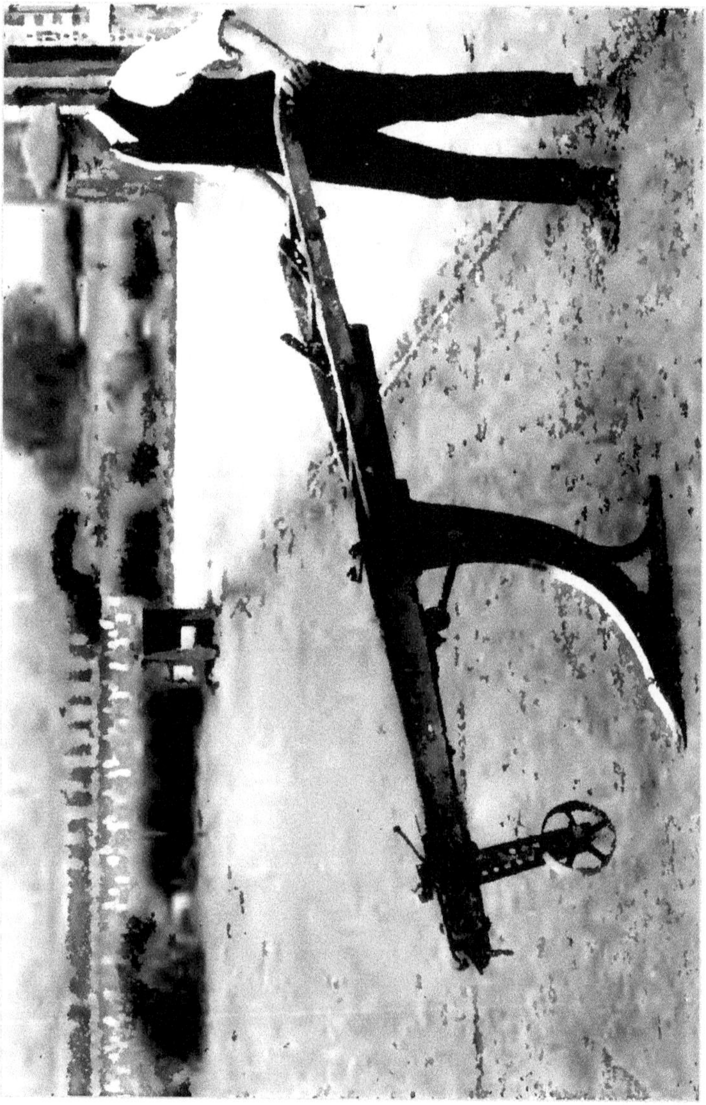

Subsoil plough

Cambridge roller

Cultivator

day should be selected for sowing, and a very useful machine is sold for this operation at quite a moderate price, called the Little Wonder Sowing Machine, which is illustrated here. An even distribution of seed can be depended upon by using it and by employing an intelligent man, who walks at an even pace up and down the quarter to be sown, pegs being used at the ends of the portion dealt with. It is better to sow twice than only once, using about two-thirds of the allotted amount in the first sowing, and then the remaining one-third across the land. If 8 bushels to the acre be used, a thick turf should be obtained quickly; and it is better, in my opinion, to use as a general rule the finest mixture of seeds, and pay more for it, than to purchase a cheaper mixture with rye grass. The comparative increase in the total cost of the construction of the course is but slight. Rye grass germinates more quickly than the finer grasses, and in some places like the Riviera this is of enormous importance, and it is advisable to use it under such circumstances; but I would prefer not to do so in England unless compelled by other reasons. The early autumn—say, the first week in September—is an excellent time to sow, and I have had better results by choosing that time than in any other period. For experimental purposes I have sown seed during almost every month of the year and, owing to exceptional weather, had some very amusing results. Another favourite time to sow is early in March. For the North of England it is better to be later in the spring than in the South. After the seed is sown the ground should be very carefully hand-raked, and the men should be watched so that they do not leave little furrows in the land from the prongs of the rakes; otherwise the grass will come up in long lines and not indiscriminately on the surface, which is what we want to see. When this has been done the surface can be heavily rolled on a dry day; the roller is generally used far too little for this process of cultivation, and, at the risk of repetition, let us remember that the firmer the seedbed the better the germination is sure to be.

Having now worked hard and taken every precaution, we shall surely be entitled to a little relaxation, and see the young plants come up and grow and flourish, and a beautiful fine sward appear in next to no time. And so we shall if we have luck; but all sorts of calamities are likely to happen. Terrific rain will possibly come upon us and wash the seed from the

Spike harrow

The "Little Wonder" Seed Sower

Edward Ray driving

Bunker at Ganton

hills to the hollows; a very severe frost may seize upon the young plants and check them badly, if not kill them; and a long spell of dry east wind may wither them, and a summer of tropical heat and record droughts may step in upon us and destroy the young turf which, to our great joy, was growing so well. In fact, the plagues of Egypt seem but slight evils in comparison with the trials sometimes experienced by the keen and anxious greenkeeper. We have all passed through some bad times in connection with new courses, and the general golfing public have never yet realised that sometimes it is not an exceedingly easy matter to turn a large area of land into perfect golfing turf in a few short months. Only constant supervision and careful nursing can bring this about, and sometimes even then the fates are against us, and we have to put up with ridiculous criticism from the owner of a small villa, who has perhaps, after many years of close attention, got a little patch of indifferent grass to grow in a sort of way in his back garden. When eventually we do succeed the result compensates us for any small irritation we may have suffered, possibly none too meekly, in the past, as, given a nice, fine, bright day in the early spring or autumn, a course like Sunningdale and others of the same description appeals to the weary man as few other things do. The green turf, with its background of heather, has a fascination to the eye which it is difficult to excel; and if the course has been "carved out," to use Mr. Croome's words, in an irregular, rugged manner, and the artificial work properly concealed, the effect is indeed pleasing. Golfers are, moreover, becoming now more and more sensitive to the artistic side of golf courses, and the man who just ploughs round in an entirely golfing spirit is getting rarer every day. I know it well from the outcry which is raised if a hole is changed and an intruding Scotch fir-tree has to be sacrificed. The old custom of squaring off the course and greens in rectangular fashion is departing, and instead we find an irregular course, with a bay of turf here and there and a promontory of heather to slightly turn the line of play to right or left as the case may be, and the result is desirable in every way. And if the heather be never levelled off, but allowed to encroach a little even on the margins, it will appear as if it were naturally growing into the turf, and the artificiality be further reduced. Everyone knows how pretty a border of flowers looks when the plants are allowed to grow over the edge and on to the paths, and the gardener's trimming instincts are checked with a firm hand. The same thing applies to heather golf courses. The margins of heather prove excellent hazards, and the sods used for the banks of bunkers are all in keeping with the character of the district. We can also employ such sods to make walls for our shelters, which, if thatched with the local plant, will enable us to avoid the erection of little suburban tea houses which so often find their way into unsuitable surroundings. Heather mounds and pots form also useful hazards, and a pleasant change from wet, congealed sand, which is so often the alternative. There is only one more point which I desire to bring forward in connection with heather courses. A thick layer of impervious ironstone often exists under the surface, and some consider that it is essential to break through this crust, commonly called "the pan," before attempting to grow turf. I have found that if drains are laid on the top of it to carry off the surplus water, very good results can be obtained, and as it is often 2 feet or more below the surface, an enormous expense is avoided.

COMMONS

Now let us consider a totally different proposition, and not nearly such a difficult one so far as the cultural part is concerned–the case of constructing a golf course on a common. If we have a large tract of good old turf growing on a light, sandy soil with gravel underneath, without the semblance of a hedge, with clumps of whin bushes, broom, and bracken, and some pleasant undulations, and one or two bold features thrown in, there is not much room for complaint, and there is a prospect of some very enjoyable golf. However, two difficulties exist–the commoners and the commonable beasts. The commoners need at times a lot of tact–the commonable beasts an even temper and considerable patience. Both are apt to resent interference with their rights; the former retaliate at times by digging up the best putting green with their spades, and the latter by destroying it with their hoofs. The best plan to get over both difficulties is to encourage the commoners to play golf themselves, and if a club be started for them, and the ways and means provided for them to enjoy the game, the manners of the commonable beasts are apt also to improve. In time an annual match can be held between the parent club and the commoners' club, and during the subsequent convivial evening leave may be obtained for making a few more necessary bunkers, even at the expense of the commonable beast. These hazards must, however, be made with discretion; otherwise a cow or a goat will be sure to fall a victim to them, and break its leg or do some other quite unnecessary and foolish thing. Then, again, pedestrians have a nasty way of objecting to being hit by a golf ball. I was called in some time ago to advise a club which had a large common at its disposal. I planned what I was pleased to think quite a good course, and left the place in the best of spirits. However, the course was never made. There was one delightful hole, which adjoined some seats used by the public to observe from a sitting posture the setting sun. It had certainly been suggested to me, and swept aside as ridiculous, that possibly some of these observers might receive a cruel blow in the back of the neck from a pulled tee shot. And in the end these seats spoilt the course, and, in addition, a beautiful hole with a ravine running parallel to catch a pulled shot, unless stopped by—a seat.

Parks

Next, probably, in order of merit comes the park course. But the park must be large, and the soil light, to enable one to lay out a good course. There is of necessity a feeling of restriction when playing the game with a 6-foot oak paling on every side, and a few roe deer grazing on the horizon do not take this away. The sense of freedom is usually one of the great charms of the game, and it is almost impossible to lay out a big, bold course in a park unless it be of large dimensions, and one needs some three or four hundred acres within the ring fence to prevent the cramped feeling. No doubt many links have been made in parks of from 100 to 150 acres; but is the same pleasure derived from a game under such conditions as from one played on a course carved out from a large heathery moor or big open common?

The boundary and the trees will probably be the most prominent difficulties in making a course of this description. The first can be got over if there is plenty of land, and it is possible to be extravagant with it and leave a margin so as to avoid constantly seeing the fence. And one can even lay out a course, if the materials be sufficient, to which the well-known term of contempt used by the superior seaside golfer, "It is just park golf," cannot be fairly applied.

Trees—The trees are, however, always a difficulty. It is hard to condemn a fine old specimen oak or beech because it comes into the line of play. At Stoke Poges one fine old beech tree caused me much unpleasantness. It was, unfortunately, right in the line of play of what has, perhaps, turned out to be a satisfactory short hole, with a certain amount of character about it. We tried our best to save the tree, but in the end there was no way out of the difficulty, and it had to go. It is a more or less accepted fact that trees are not the best of hazards, for the obvious reason that they unfortunately afford but slight opportunity for the display of golfing skill in extricating the ball from their clutches. Moreover, during the fall of the leaf they are always a nuisance, and it is exceedingly difficult to grow satisfactory turf under their shade; but they are undoubtedly charming features in a landscape view.

General Treatment—On the other hand, there are usually many desirable characteristics in this class of course. The turf, if well rolled down and cut close, works up very quickly, and if the soil be light, it almost becomes too good for the game; but old turf of this description will stand a vast amount of heavy rolling between the greens, and a motor-roller is very useful for the work. There are generally many pleasant-looking undulations and ravines, and almost invariably some water hazards, although, with the present heavy balls and their equally heavy price, the latter are not always acceptable to the bad player, nor to the good one as far as that goes. Abundance of land, light soil, old turf, good drainage, and a few bold features should give an opportunity of making a good course. If there be lakes of many acres in extent, there will be some difficulty in knowing how to deal with them, as it is not much use to ask the long-handicap player to lose 2*s*. 6*d*. balls every day of his life. But very often it is possible so to place the hole that the timorous can skirt round the margin, and the player full of natural or artificial courage can "go" for the long carry. Thus the big feature will not be lost to the golf course, and the path of safety provides an answer to the complaint from the loser of new golf balls.

Clay Courses

Now, with many variations, we gradually descend to the last resort of the keen golfer—heavy clay. I have just returned from bunkering such a course. After rising at 5:45 a.m. and missing my train in London owing to the railway line being blocked somewhere below Sunningdale, I arrived an hour and a half late on the scene of operations. A blizzard was blowing from the east, snow was driving into our faces, and the state of the ground was—well, it was wet. A committee of enthusiasts followed me round, and I put in pegs mercilessly, until at last we came to a flat piece of ground about 120 yards long, where a short hole had previously been determined upon. I had not the honour of laying out the course. I let loose the imprisoned venom which was in me, and after bunkering the hole in every possible direction we went in to lunch, and I particularly remember how warm and soothing was a bottle of Pommard, which my kind hosts provided. But I have seen many worse courses than the one in question, and can quite understand the feelings of a visitor to a strange club who, on being asked what he thought of the links, replied that they might have been much worse; and on being further questioned as to what he meant, answered: "Well, you see, there might have been eighteen holes instead of only nine!"

After spending several hours of a raw winter's day in wearily plodding over flat fields with high bullfinch hedges, with one's boots wet through and twice their normal size from gradual accumulations of clay, one is inclined to lose heart and to stop the proposed attempt to play the game within a radius of at least twenty miles from the spot. Some would, no doubt, do this, and at the same time deprive innumerable golfers of ever playing, except during a brief summer holiday. With a clean sweep of the hedges, careful drainage, and good bunkering, an extraordinary change can be effected, especially if whin bushes or clumps of broom can be grown here and there to relieve the monotony and to break up the flatness; so much so that even a fastidious seaside player may enjoy a game there on a nice warm day in the spring, when the putting greens have become fast and firm owing to the care of a good greenkeeper, and the course has been worked up by rolling and mowing.

But everything depends upon the actual constructive work of such a course. If this has been carried out well and the bunkering made to look as natural as possible, and bath-like pits avoided and nice rugged mounds made, and not a series of pepper-pots or ant-heaps, it is quite possible to play several most enjoyable rounds over such a course during many months of the year, but not during a blizzard from the east in the month of January. What has already been said about drainage and obtaining a porous, firm surface applies especially to clay courses. Cinders can also be used under the turf on the greens; it is, no doubt, as old as the hills, but has hardly been done sufficiently in the construction of golf courses.

Forest Courses

A few years ago no one would have thought of constructing a golf course in a forest, and probably the New Zealand Club's links at Byfleet was the first example. But since then there have been several successful instances both at home and abroad, and some notes about the clearing of the site may be useful.

It is essential to make the clearing bold and wide, as it is not very enjoyable to play down long alleys with trees on either side, and better effects can be obtained from a landscape point of view if this be done. It will be necessary to grub up most of the roots through the course, but a few sparsely scattered ones can be turned into mounds and expense saved, as grubbing is very costly. At the Swinley Forest golf course we cut down about 14,000, and of these some 5,000 were grubbed. I think almost every known method was tried, and with small trees we ground, but only those on the far side to the engine, as when the tree fell the large side branches would get fixed in the earth, and act as effectual brakes to all the efforts of the engine. These roots had afterwards to be grubbed, and meant a large extra expense. The cost of pulling down by the engine, including hire, coal, labour, etc., came to about 1*s*. per tree; but the subsequent cost of grubbing the roots of the big trees and getting them out of their holes was enormous in comparison—in fact, so big that I prefer not to mention it. We tried everything

Swinley Forest: Felling timber (1st view)

Swinley Forest: Felling timber (2nd view)

Swinley Forest, 12 months after sowing

—patent root extractors, blasting, haulage by horses, scientific levers, and goodness only knows what else—but had to return always to the British workman with his mattock. The trees by the side of the course need not be grubbed, but can be cut practically level with the surface of the ground by means of cross-cut saws. The stumps can then be bored by drills, of about 2 inches in diameter; saltpetre is then placed in the holes and they are filled up with a little water and corked. After two or three months or so the corks can be removed and the holes filled with paraffin and then set on fire; by this means the stumps will gradually smoulder away. I am indebted for this information to my friend Mr. Hudson, of *Country Life.*

Chapter II

The Formation and Maintenance of Putting Greens and Teeing Grounds

By Martin H. F. Sutton, F.L.S.

Many are the considerations which arise when the construction of a golf course is in contemplation, but it may be maintained that nothing is of more importance than the position and formation of putting greens and teeing grounds. With their position I have nothing to do, since that question comes within the scope of golf architecture, and is dealt with in this book by Mr. H. S. Colt, who has made the subject peculiarly his own.

With regard, however, to their formation and maintenance, it will be readily conceded that there is one common necessity for both—a perfectly firm surface. By this is not meant a hard, harsh surface, but one that does not "poach" in weather unsuitable for golf. The moment one walks on a firm green it is easy to form an opinion from the feel of the turf whether its firmness is due to over-rolling or to the employment of more correct methods. If the latter, there is nothing harsh about it; but it is porous as well as firm, and possibly just a little gritty from a recent application of sea sand. It is always a pleasure to walk on greens of this character, especially when, even in bad-weather conditions, they are behaving properly, as they assuredly will do if the attention they have received has not only been correct but thorough.

Golfers are sometimes a little unreasonable, for they expect to play in all sorts of weather, and happy indeed must be the secretary or the greenkeeper who, on a really bad day, is commended for his greens. It is, however, an unusual occurrence, for, like the cox. of a university or college crew, he is more accustomed to "all kicks and no ha'pence."

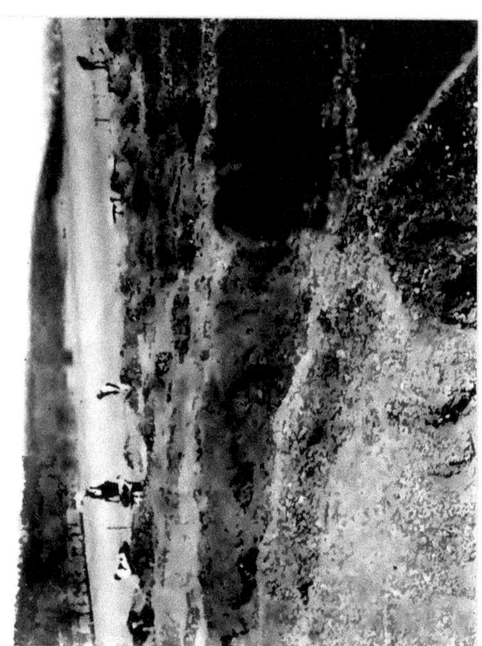

Preparing a putting green

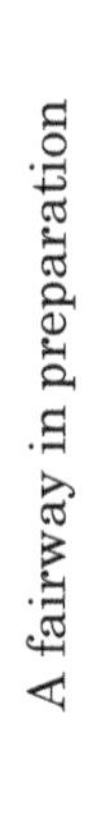

A fairway in preparation

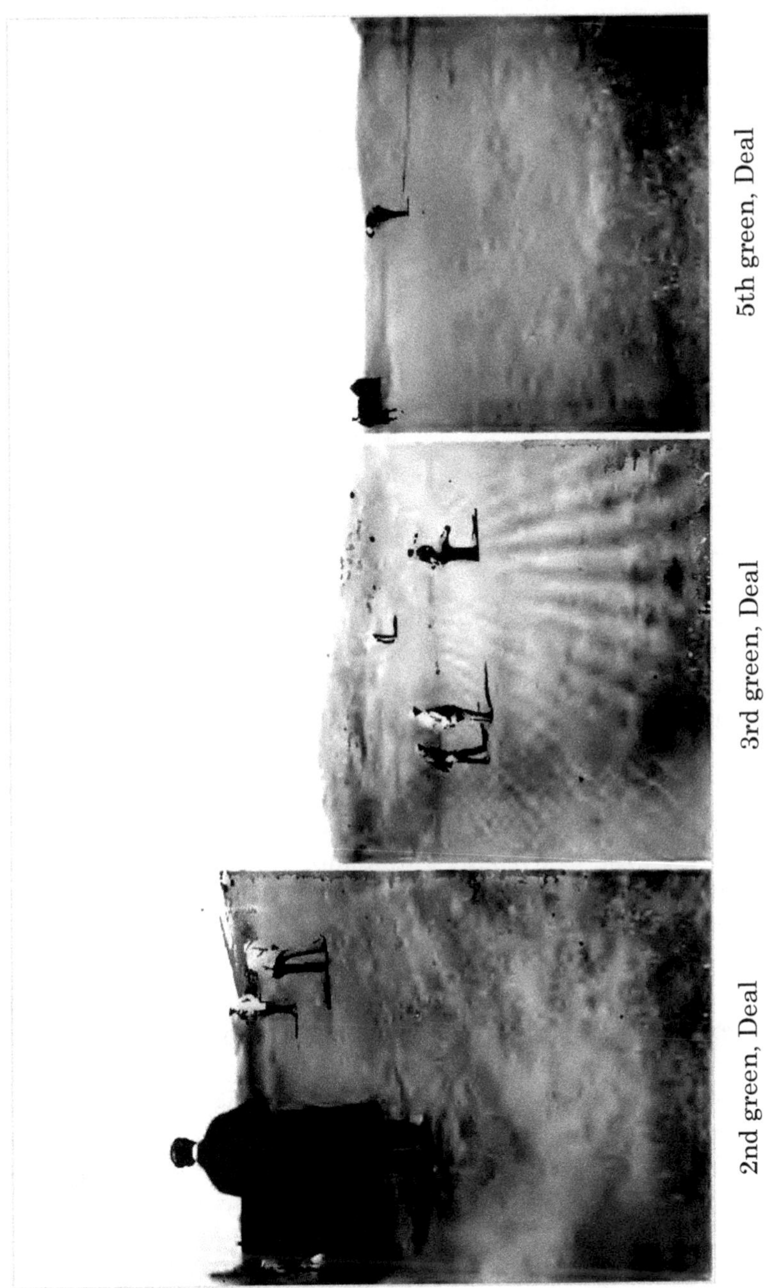

2nd green, Deal

3rd green, Deal

5th green, Deal

If the cricket pitch is wet, the umpires veto play for the day and return to the pavilion; yet it is no uncommon sight on a suburban golf course near London to see 300 or 400 people, caddies included, in a single day walking across a comparatively small area of turf, when the surface is like putty, during a thaw with the frost not yet out of the ground. In fairness to the turf, courses ought really to be closed under such circumstances, though it is quite easy to understand the impossibility of doing so.

But, apart from frosts and thaws and hail and snow, and such-like weather "samples" which our American friends good-humouredly accuse us of indulging in, how are we to get the proper firmness so that the greens will be in good order during wet weather? It must certainly not be done entirely with the roller; for if over-rolling is resorted to, the surface will assuredly cake in places, and the result will be bare patches and consequent annoyance.

Drainage is the first thing to attend to. If a water supply is laid on to the greens, it is hardly possible to overdrain them, and except where it is situated on a plateau or a slope, or there is a gravel subsoil within a foot or so of the surface, it will be better to "herringbone" each green in the first place, and not wait for it to get wet and soft, and finally sour. When this has been done care should be taken to see that the water percolates quickly through the surface to the pipes by incorporating gritty material, such as coke breeze, charcoal, or sand, to keep the soil porous. This is without doubt more than half the secret of successful greenkeeping—the getting rid of surplus water in the quickest manner possible.

It is next necessary to consider the vexed question of turfing versus sowing, and long experience goes to show that, unless quite exceptionally good turf be procurable, both greens and tees should, in the best interests of the club, be sown. It is specially desirable in the case of heather courses, as it is then possible to obtain a perfectly clean seedbed, and a mixture of fine-leaved varieties of grass sown under such conditions will give within a year a much better covering of turf than can be secured the other way.

In the case of meadow land and old pastures it is naturally more difficult to obtain a really clean seedbed, owing to the seeds of indigenous weeds which are blown about from the surrounding herbage, and which continue to settle on the area to be sown after, perhaps, two or three crops of weeds have been cleaned off. Some idea of the difficulties of the greenkeeper in this respect may be gathered when it is remembered that it has been computed that every square yard of soil contains weed seeds varying in quantity from 2,000 to 34,000. On the other hand, as has been already stated, it is a rare occurrence to obtain really clean fine turf, and to form a green of turf composed of ordinary meadow herbage needs mention only to be at once pronounced impracticable. At the best it would take years to "fine down" the character of the herbage, and good greens are essential to every club possessing any ambition whatever. It is clear, therefore, that in nine cases out of ten greens must be sown, and allowance made for a more thorough and continuous system of hand-weeding than is necessary in the case, for instance, of heather courses.

Fine grasses, of which putting green mixtures are composed, germinate and develop somewhat slowly, whereas weeds grow very rapidly, especially in the spring months; but when once the young turf is enabled to form a close sward it will be found that if the weeds have been kept down in the earlier stages, they will afterwards give but comparatively little trouble.

The young, tender blades of grass will not, of course, bear the treading and tramping of boots, and therefore weeding should be done from planks laid across the green, and moved down the surface as each drift, so to speak, is cleared.

Where, under exceptional circumstances, financial or otherwise, it is impossible to sow, and there is no alternative to using local turf for greens and tees, a certain amount of improvement can be obtained by renovating the turf with fine grass seeds, constant eradication of the more conspicuous weeds, and repeated dressings of fine sea sand. It is only in recent years that the value of the last named has been realised, and it is remarkable indeed to see what can be accomplished through its judicious use. It is often supposed that its extraordinary power of "fining" grass is attributable to the saline property it contains; and as it is composed to some extent of minute atoms of broken shell, there appears to be ground for the assumption.

When a firm surface has been obtained on greens or tees the chief difficulty to overcome is to secure and retain a smooth, even plant of grass. Putting greens need constant observation and unremitting attention. The greens on a course will vary largely in character, and each will possess, in fact, a certain amount of individuality which must be studied, and even various parts of the same green may quite possibly need entirely different treatment. As a case in point, one may take a well-known green on a famous championship course in Scotland, the soil of one portion of which near the burn is moist, rich loam, while the upper portion near the hummocks at the back is very much lighter in character. The grass on the first portion needs no manure, and only constant light applications of sand to prevent it from becoming too luxuriant, while the farther part will probably require both manure and water. Thus it is impossible to prescribe in a general way for the needs of putting greens, beyond stating what is an obvious fact—that as soon as the grass shows any signs of flagging the first opportunity should be taken of giving it some help with a suitable fertiliser.

It has been abundantly demonstrated at Rothamsted what divergent results can be obtained from treating identical plots of turf in the same field with different artificial fertilisers for prolonged periods, and I have myself secured quite astonishing changes in the composition of turf in a large area, even in four or five years only, from certain manurial dressings. I must not, however, discuss this question at any length, as it forms the subject of an article in this work by Mr. A. D. Hall, who is of all men most competent to deal with it. Suffice it to say that, given the necessary experience and data to work upon, turf not only benefits greatly from the application of suitable fertilisers, but may be changed in character almost at will by skilful treatment.

When once a green possesses a fine plant of grass a distinct point has been gained, but unremitting care will be required to keep it, and it is always a battle to do so. Weeds come and have to be destroyed by lawn sand or chemicals, or to be removed by hand. Then worms arrive on the scene, and, in spite of their advocates (there are still a few), it is necessary to kill them off with a ruthless hand. The worm-killer will do this effectually if used on a warm, muggy day with plenty of water. They arrive on the surface in huge numbers, and can be brushed into heaps and carried off in the wheelbarrow. It is necessary, however, to warn club secretaries and greenkeepers as to the risks which

Guide Worm (to Mr. and Mrs. Tourist ditto): There you behold the field on which fell in a single day 25,000 of our best blue-blooded worm nobility in the famous Sutton Massacre!

7th green, Stoke Poges

are entailed by the use of poisons for this purpose; they may be effective, but I have seen the turf on first-class greens destroyed and the soil poisoned by their use, and in view of the very efficacious worm-destroyers now obtainable, which are not only non-poisonous but actually beneficial to the turf, there is no reason why dangerous preparations should be any longer employed. In addition to earthworms, pests such as eelworms and other noxious grubs may appear in the soil; the former are now very much on the increase, and likely to do great damage unless dealt with as soon as their presence becomes known. Sulphate of potash, at the rate of one ounce to the square yard, has proved effectual in checking them. Eelworms create much havoc at times, and as they are so minute as to be unobservable except under a microscope, the real cause of the loss of turf is in many cases quite unknown. Leather-jacket grubs, the first stage of the daddy-longlegs fly, are also sometimes a nuisance. Birds, however, will destroy them in great measure, and if we see the marks of their beaks in the turf, we get a hint that the grubs may be present in large numbers. A worm-killer will prove effective in their eradication, and a heavy roller has also been found useful.

A few notes on three matters of routine—cutting, rolling, and watering—may perhaps be of service here. On many up-to-date courses it is a rule to cut the grass whenever there is anything to remove. Some greenkeepers hesitate to use a machine in winter, and in consequence the grass is allowed to grow to such an extent as to make accurate putting almost impossible. Newly formed turf naturally requires special care; but in the case of well-established turf it is a mistake to be sparing with the mower, and it should be further remembered that grass allowed to grow unchecked is liable to become coarse and lose its fine character. In a normal season there are, as a matter of fact, comparatively few weeks in the year when there can be said to be no growth at all. A friend of mine, the secretary of an important course in the South, says with reference to winter mowing: "Throughout a period of years I have never yet seen damage arise from cutting, and we use machines set close to the surface. In very dry weather the blades are raised slightly—about half an inch, I should think."

The growth of grass during winter naturally varies greatly according to the weather; but when at all pronounced it should certainly be got rid of, and it is desirable under such circumstances to use boxes on the machines to collect the cuttings. It is true a somewhat valuable manure is lost thereby; but if the cuttings are left on the ground, the worms are almost certain to increase, and, if wanted, manure can, after all, be added in a more desirable form. In a dry summer, when worms are no longer a nuisance, the boxes may often, of course, be left in the toolshed, as a large quantity of decayed vegetation is thus added to the soil, while on poor, sandy soil, where worm-casts are almost unknown, the boxes may be kept off all the year round.

Heavy rolling has now gone out of fashion, and the old method of flattening out the worm-casts into little muddy cakes over the whole surface of the greens is seldom met with. Light rollers are largely used, and if weighing not more than a hundredweight, and of a width of, say, 36 inches, do no harm. It is useless to roll in very dry weather; a heavy rolling when the ground is not wet, only just soft, will do good from time to time. But the surface of the greens should never be in the least degree caked by this work, and it ought not to be necessary to employ the heavy roller more than half a dozen times in the year.

The summer of 1911 brought the necessity of water for putting greens to the notice of every greenkeeper, and for some weeks, wherever available, it was probably in use day and night. It is supposed by many to be dangerous to use the hose in the middle of a hot August day with a blazing sun overhead; but experience has proved that no harm is done, provided the green is kept moist until evening. If it were possible to apply moisture to all the greens of a course every night, then no doubt the watering in the day time could be omitted with advantage; but it is practically impossible to do this, and water given during the day is better than none at all. It should, however, be remembered that a half-hearted sprinkling is useless, and in point of fact harmful, as it causes the roots of the grass to work towards the surface instead of striking down deep in search of moisture, and they consequently get scorched and the plants are killed. A strong pressure, sufficient to keep two large sprinklers at work on three or four greens at the same time, is what should be aimed at, though to many this will seem but a

16th tee, Rye

Stoke Poges, 1st tee Massy driving

counsel of perfection outside the realms of possibility. Where no supply is available there is, of course, nothing to be done until a drought breaks; but if the turf has not been actually destroyed, much may then be achieved by judicious feeding. Greens which have been heavily watered will also need help in this direction, especially if they have been flooded, as a certain amount of nourishment will have been washed away. When newly sown putting greens or tees are so unfortunate as to be caught by a prolonged dry period, it is an excellent plan to protect the young grass by a thin dressing of rape meal or malt culms, which to a considerable degree shields it from the sun's rays. Peat moss litter is better still, but it requires very careful use, or the grass will be smothered. It should be finely screened to remove all matted lumps, and, in addition, should be disturbed every few days with the rake to ensure circulation of the air. And here it may be mentioned in passing that peat moss litter, when used with discrimination, has proved particularly valuable for incorporating with soil consisting of pure sand, where without its aid it would be impossible to establish fine turf. It is comparatively cheap, and it provides just the consistency of material necessary for the development of the root action of fine grasses.

In watering turf it is always best to employ sprinklers if possible, as when the nozzle of the hose is used, if the pressure is good, the rush of water is liable to wash away the soil from the grass and even expose the roots. Mention may also be made of the necessity of giving a heavier dressing of water to banks round greens and to ridges than to hollows; the latter will look after themselves, but the ridges in undulating greens are seldom granted the amount of water they need, while they are naturally the first portions of the green to be caught by the sun's rays.

Even in the case of the best-managed courses, where the greens receive unlimited care and attention, turf may be destroyed in places either by over-wear or by great heat, and under such circumstances patching will have to be resorted to. While it is important to have plenty of root-growth in the turf used for this purpose, it is desirable that it should be cut moderately thin—say, about 2 inches—since thick turf does not start

Chapter III

The Manuring of Golf Greens and Courses

By A. D. Hall, F.R.S.

It might almost be taken as an axiom that the grass of nearly all golf courses, whether seaside or inland, especially on the greens, will require regular manuring, and observation of many golf courses that have been in existence for the last quarter of a century only tends to confirm this conclusion. In the first place the soil is nearly always very poor to start with, and both before and after its conversion into golf links it will have received no assistance, but have been steadily impoverished. On the true sand links it is obvious that the soil contains the minimum of nutrition, and even inland golf links are usually laid out on the lightest and thinnest of soils, very commonly soils that have always been too poor to be worth bringing into cultivation, and have therefore remained in the state of open heath or common. It is only in the neighbourhood of populous centres, where golf links have to be put down on whatever land is available, that we ever find a course laid out on what a farmer would describe as a good pasture. Furthermore, the treatment the land receives only tends to impoverish it. Suppose the grass is kept down by sheep, though the losses may be small, they are still continuous. We may calculate that, roughly, nine-tenths of the fertilising constituents contained in the grass that is eaten by the sheep get returned to the land and help to grow grass again; but still one-tenth of the plant food in the grass is being taken away, and this proportion is likely to be increased when, as is usually the case, the land is grazed by a breeding flock and young lambs are making their flesh and bone at the expense of the food in the soil. If, as is nowadays so often the case, the grass, even in the fairway of the course, has to be regularly cut and the cuttings are removed, then the losses are even greater. We may take it that repeated cuttings of the springing grass to keep it close will take away far more from the soil than will a crop of hay, because it is just during its early growth that the grass contains a maximum of fertilising constituents, and any farmer knows how it would impoverish his land to remove a hay crop year after year without putting anything back to feed the land. On a green, the cutting process is most close and continuous, and only rarely is the cut grass allowed to lie and so find its way back to the soil. A series of cuttings of an ordinary inland lawn in a poorish condition gave the following results for the nitrogen, phosphoric acid, and potash removed in successive cuttings during the first two months only of the season, and that a dry one, and when we realise that a crop of 2 tons of hay to the acre would only remove 66 lb. of nitrogen, 17 lb. of phosphoric acid, and 75 lb. of potash, we see what a heavy tax is being put upon the resources of the soil on which a well-kept green is maintained.

CONSTITUENTS REMOVED IN SUCCESSIVE CUTTINGS OF A LAWN, LB. PER ACRE.

<table>
<tr><th>Date of Cutting</th><th>Dry Matter</th><th>Nitrogen</th><th>Phosphoric Acid</th><th>Potash</th></tr>
<tr><td>March 14th</td><td>247</td><td>11.0</td><td>2.4</td><td>6.1</td></tr>
<tr><td>" 29th</td><td>142</td><td>5.8</td><td>1.5</td><td>3.4</td></tr>
<tr><td>April 16th</td><td>216</td><td>6.7</td><td>1.8</td><td>4.4</td></tr>
<tr><td>" 26th</td><td>94</td><td>2.9</td><td>0.8</td><td>1.9</td></tr>
<tr><td>May 3rd</td><td>51</td><td>1.5</td><td rowspan="4">2.5</td><td rowspan="4">7.0</td></tr>
<tr><td>" 10th</td><td>101</td><td>3.2</td></tr>
<tr><td>" 17th</td><td>79</td><td>2.6</td></tr>
<tr><td>" 24th</td><td>47</td><td>1.6</td></tr>
<tr><td>Total</td><td>977</td><td>35.3</td><td>9.0</td><td>22.8</td></tr>
</table>

There is only one remedy for the progressive deterioration that must set in, and that is the use of appropriate fertilisers. The use of manure of any kind upon golf links, and especially upon the greens, is often objected to on the plea that it will render the grass rank and coarse; but, assuming that the links have been made out of anything but rich inland pasture, there is not the slightest probability that such a result will ever be attained. The soil itself prevents it, for the sandy land upon which the true links are situated will never hold enough water to permit of the growth of rank grass, however abundant the food supply. On such courses it is only in wet seasons and in the hollows to which the drainage naturally gravitates that we ever see long grass, showing that it is the abundant water supply rather than the presence or absence of the fertiliser which causes such luxuriant growth. Moreover, the constant cutting would not permit any coarse grass to establish itself, because, as will be emphasised later, in the struggle for existence that goes on in a patch of turf only those plants survive which can accommodate themselves to the prevailing circumstances, whether of food, water supply, or treatment, and any coarse tufted or tall-growing grass is bound to suffer and be crowded out when the conditions necessitate life below the level of the lawn mower's blades.

In considering the action of fertilisers upon grassland, two distinct things have to be taken into account—the actual feeding of the plant for the particular purpose in view, and the alteration of the botanical character of the herbage which can be effected by adjusting the composition of the fertiliser. When we look closely at a meadow or lawn we see that it by no means consists entirely of grass, but is a mixture of a number of different species of grass with various kinds of clover and a large range of other species of plants which we may briefly group together as weeds. All these species are struggling to increase and extend their borders, and the constitution of the herbage, which for a given type of soil remains fairly constant from year to year, represents the state of balance which has been attained in the struggle between the competing plants. If the conditions are altered in any way by a change of food or water supply, some or other of the species will derive a comparative advantage and begin to spread at the expense of their less-favoured neighbours, until after a time a very different population is established, and the whole aspect of the vegetation is changed. How far variations of manuring can bring about such changes is most clearly demonstrated by the historic grass field at Rothamsted, where certain plots of old grassland, all alike at the beginning of the experiment, have for over fifty years been receiving different combinations of fertiliser, the same treatment being given to the same plots year after year. The plots are now absolutely unlike one another, and look as though they might have been carved out of different counties and set side by side, although no seed has ever been sown, and the changes have been slowly brought about in response to the different manuring. For example, the plot which has had no manure carries a very variegated herbage, in which as many as forty-seven species are to be found. Of late years the weeds have been chiefly prominent, until they constitute nearly one-half the whole herbage by weight. The most abundant grasses are the quaking grass, so characteristic of poor land, and sheep's fescue, while the clovers make up only 7 or 8 percent of the total. Adjoining this is a plot which has received sulphate of ammonia and superphosphate every year, and on this there are only fifteen species, while 95 percent of the whole herbage consists of grass, clovers being entirety absent. Close by is another plot receiving phosphates and potash but no nitrogen, and here the clovers make up more than one-third of the weight of the material that is removed by cutting. On another plot, again, with a complete manure rich in nitrogen, the species are reduced to ten, of which three coarse grasses are alone of any account, making up as much as 97 percent of the whole herbage. Now these plots are cut for hay every year, and so are not strictly comparable to a green; but the principles which may be deduced from the examination equally apply to herbage that is kept short, and we can briefly set out what those lessons are. In the first place we see from the unmanured plot that the impoverishment produced by continued cutting without any fertiliser results in weeds, because the weeds are, on the whole, more hardy than the grass, and the very varied vegetation is able to fit in together and utilise to the full whatever food is available. For example, two species with roots occupying different layers of the soil, which therefore hardly compete with one another, are together better able to cover a given piece of poor soil than either of them singly. Grass, especially the finer varieties, only seems able to keep the land to itself when there is plenty of food available. In another way the same principle is illustrated by the prevalence of moss upon the unmanured plot during the winter time. This moss is only a sign of poverty; it is perhaps the least exacting form of vegetation, and it seizes upon the bare patches of soil between the grasses and other plants when they die down in the autumn, although it becomes crowded out and disappears from sight when growth is renewed in the early summer. Moss of this kind is very common on certain golf links throughout the winter and early spring, especially upon the seaside soils and on very thin chalk land. It is often supposed that moss is a sign of wetness or sourness of the soil, but though there are some kinds which flourish in swampy places or under the drip and shade of trees, the particular species which invades golf links is always most abundant in the driest and airiest situations, and may be found coating pure chalk where no possible trace of acidity can remain. Such moss is purely and simply an accompaniment of impoverishment, and indicates the fact that the soil is too poor to sustain enough grass to keep the surface covered during those times of the year when growth is at a minimum. It will have been noticed by many people how excessively mossy many links were during the winter and early spring of 1911-12, because of the immense amount of damage done to the grass by the preceding summer's drought. Various experiments have been made to see how such moss can best be eradicated; but though it may be killed off temporarily with certain chemicals, the only permanent cure is to get the land rich enough to cover itself with grass and to keep the surface in good order by harrowing and rolling.

The next fact of importance is the differential action of incomplete manures. It is true that all plants have to be fed with the same nitrogen, phosphoric acid, and potash, but they differ very much in their powers of obtaining one or other of these constituents from natural resources, and therefore what is an incomplete fertiliser for one plant may furnish all the requirements of another, because it is able to supply itself with the missing link from the soil. For example, we find that where no nitrogen is contained in the fertiliser, but plenty of lime, potash, and phosphoric acid, the clovers and other leguminous plants grow with great vigour and tend to become dominant in the herbage. This is because the clovers, unlike other plants, are able to derive the necessary nitrogen from the atmosphere, and therefore can make up a complete manure for themselves when they are supplied with minerals like potash and phosphoric acid, whereas grass is very little better off for an unlimited supply of the two latter constituents if the indispensable nitrogen be not also furnished in the fertiliser. It is true that the growth of clover in the end promotes the growth of grass, because the clover gathers nitrogen from the atmosphere, and as it dies and decays leaves this nitrogen behind in the soil for the benefit of other plants. Still, such a process is slow, and rarely concerns us on a golf links. Speaking generally, the greenkeeper wishes to discourage clovers rather than otherwise; especially are they to be avoided on the greens themselves. On the fairway of the course there is not so much objection to the presence of the very fine creeping clovers that alone flourish upon proper links soil. Clover is soft, and does not wear as well as grass proper; but the ball sits up fairly on it, and it is of value in improving the fertility of the soil and building up a turf, because of its power of gathering nitrogen from the atmosphere. For this reason, on the poorest and thinnest soils, as on seaside links and sandy heaths, it is desirable to encourage a reasonable growth of clover, though it must be kept off the greens. The experiments show that to get clover to grow quickly we must apply both phosphates and potash; without the two we shall not get the clover, although lime, especially upon heavy soils, will sometimes act like potash, because the lime unlocks some of the resources of insoluble potash contained in practically all soils. Speaking generally, the use of potash manures should be avoided on the golf links, and lime or fertilisers containing lime, such as basic slag, must be used with discretion; on the greens in particular no fertiliser containing potash should ever be used. If the mineral manures promote growth of clovers, on the other hand nitrogen, in all its forms, promotes the growth of grass, and we may learn from the Rothamsted plots that the ground may be made to cover itself exclusively with grass by the use of nitrogen fertilisers alone without any weeding. We must, however, distinguish between the different forms of nitrogenous fertilisers. Of those containing nothing but nitrogen, we have three which are in general use—nitrate of soda, sulphate of ammonia, and soot, though the two latter may be taken together, because the soot owes its fertilising power to the small proportion of ammonia that it contains. The two highly soluble and concentrated compounds—nitrate of soda and sulphate of ammonia—are very different in their action upon grassland. The nitrate of soda remains soluble and sinks down in the soil, so that it is found to promote the development of strong deep-rooting grasses and tap-rooted plants, whereas the sulphate of ammonia is held up near the surface and favours the shallow-rooting grasses like Sheep's Fescue, Sweet Vernal, Fiorin and other forms of Agrostis, Poas, etc. Clearly, then, sulphate of ammonia is the nitrogenous manure for the golf links and not nitrate of soda. There are a large number of other fertilisers containing more or less nitrogen, mixed, as a rule, with a varying percentage of phosphoric acid, and perhaps of potash also, thus making up a complete fertiliser. Of these, malt culms, Peruvian guano, and the so-called fish or meat guanos may be extremely useful, their great merit being that they are slower and more continuous in their action than is sulphate of ammonia.

One other general question is of importance—the amount of lime in the soil. It is necessary to keep just enough to prevent the development of acidity, which is always followed by an indifferent growth of grass with dead patches between and ultimate sterility; yet if we have an excess of lime, we run the danger of encouraging the development of clover. As to acidity, one of the Rothamsted plots shows very clearly that the continuous use of sulphate of ammonia sets up an acid condition in the soil, and that as a consequence the grass becomes very unhealthy, and in a trying time like last summer will die off in large patches. Of the soils we have to deal with on golf links, we will assume that on the seaside links there will not be much danger of acidity, because the sea sand always contains a certain proportion of broken shell, which is mainly carbonate of lime, sufficient to keep the soil in a healthy condition for a long time. Many of the light inland soils, however, contain no carbonate of lime, and may be in an actually acid condition to start with. This is generally the case on the sandy heaths, as, for example, on the Bagshot Sands on which so many of the links in West Surrey have been laid out, and the acid condition may be recognised without any further test wherever we notice that the soil is black and slightly peaty, and the sand near the surface is bleached. Again, many of the clay soils are short of carbonate of lime; indeed, it is only on the chalk downs, among inland links, that we may be quite safe from any danger of acidity. Assuming that lime will be required, it may be applied in several forms. We may use ground quicklime (ground because it is easier to apply in a fine state); but quicklime in any form is rather too rapid in its action for light soils, and it is safer to use one of the forms of finely divided carbonate of lime, which is the compound into which quicklime is rapidly converted as soon as it is placed on the soil. A suitable carbonate of lime can be obtained in some parts of the country as ground limestone, in the South as ground chalk, or, perhaps best of all, in the very finely divided residue from the water-softening process which many water companies who draw their supply from deep wells in the chalk can furnish.

Having thus disposed of the principles underlying the action of fertilisers upon grass, we may now turn to certain practical recommendations. First of all, let us deal with greens on light soil or sand. Perhaps the best general fertiliser is a dressing of good Peruvian guano, which has been found by experience to answer extremely well on all soils of this class—e.g., on the rye links. It requires no mixing, can be readily sown, soon washes into the soil, and, though it is more expensive than some of the other manures, the area to be dealt with is so small that the cost need not be considered. A guano should be selected containing 8 or 9 percent of ammonia (the composition varies from cargo to cargo), and it should be obtained from a reputable dealer or directly from the importers. It should be sown at the rate of 1 lb. per 10 square yards in February or early March, and it may be mixed with sand or light, dry soil to ensure an even distribution. It is, of course, best to sow when rain is imminent, so that it may be quickly washed into the soil. If the green shows any tendency to grow clover, we may adopt as an alternative a mixture of one part of sulphate of ammonia and two parts of superphosphate. Such may be obtained ready mixed from a manure dealer, and should be sown at the same rate (1 lb. per 10 square yards) in the early spring as above indicated. This combination possesses an acid character, and though extremely effective in discouraging clovers and promoting a growth of exactly the right grasses, it would ultimately injure the soil if persisted in, except upon pure chalk soils. It is therefore necessary also to use occasional dressings of carbonate of lime. One of the finely ground forms of carbonate of lime mentioned above should be obtained and sown at the rate of ¼ lb. per square yard any time between October and January—but the earlier the better—in alternate years. Such a dressing will preserve the soil in a healthy condition without encouraging the inroads of clover. The carbonate of lime must not be put on at the same time as the other manures, but should first have been washed into the soil.

When dealing with greens on heavy soils, and especially on clays, one of the first essentials is to try to lighten the texture of the surface. This can be effected by continual dressings of sand and powdered charcoal or coke breeze; but carbonate of lime will also be a great help, and the dressing specified above (¼ lb. per square yard) may be put on every autumn or early winter. The lime will be found to effect a slow alteration in the clay that will permit of better drainage. On greens situated on heavy soil the manuring should not be guano, but the mixture of sulphate of ammonia and superphosphate described above. If the land is naturally rich and carries rather a fat growth of grasses mixed with plenty of clover, sulphate of ammonia at the rate of ½ oz. per square yard had better be used for some years, only adding the superphosphate when the grass has begun to look rather fine drawn.

When it comes to dealing with the fairway of the course a little more discretion must be used as to whether manure is wanted or not, and the treatment can only be settled by a careful examination of the herbage. On many otherwise fine seaside links the skin of vegetation covering the sand is very thin and easily damaged, and on examination will be found to contain more weeds than grass, together with a good deal of moss. This is due to the fact that the land has been reclaimed from the sea for no great length of time, and no depth of vegetable soil has had time to accumulate, or, again, that the particular part of the course is especially subject to drought, so that the vegetation gets a very poor chance. Such a skin will stand no wear, and easily tears up under an iron club shot, leaving a wound that heals very slowly and may even begin to let the sand blow. In all these cases much better and cheaper results can be obtained by steadily manuring the thin existing skin of vegetation than by attempting to returf, especially if the turf has to be brought from another and heavier class of soil. Nothing is more disastrous than to transplant turf from heavy land on to pure sand. The vegetation dies because water cannot be drawn to it from below as it will when soil and subsoil form one continuous bed even of sand. The clay shrinks and cracks; at last you are left with a bare and muddy surface where previously there was at least clean sand beneath the weeds and moss. Manure, however, will bring on the grasses and form a layer of vegetation, which at first may dwindle in the droughts, but will strengthen from year to year as the treatment is renewed, until a respectable mat of roots is formed that will stand a good deal of hard usage and retain its life even through a bad season.

On many of the seaside links attempts are made to improve the fertility of the fairway by dressing it from time to time with mixtures of soil and farmyard manure, which have been stored up together and turned over occasionally until the manure is well rotted. This process is undoubtedly effective in building up a soil, but it has great drawbacks. In the first place it is very expensive, as may be found by calculating what a load of this compost costs in labour, cartage, etc., by the time it is spread upon the links. We may safely say that it will be as expensive as a purchased manure of ten times its fertilising value, and so exclusively nitrogenous is the compost that it tends to grow a soft, fat grass. Secondly, the soil that is applied is no real gain to the links, although it certainly adds consistency and water-retaining power; in fact, if it were persisted in, we should obtain a loam instead of a pure sandy soil. This consistency, however, is purchased at the cost of making the surface of the course muddy in winter where previously there was only pure, clean sand, and on certain seaside links the pleasure of playing in changeable weather has been distinctly depreciated since the practice of continual dressings with soil has been set on foot. The dressing itself takes some time to wash in, and puts parts of the course out of action for weeks together. A better way of building up a drought-resisting layer is to grow a thick skin of grass on the pure sand, until the mat of roots does the water-retaining necessary to keep the plant alive through a spell of dry weather; and fertilisers alone will bring this about. For this purpose, perhaps, the best fertiliser is Peruvian guano at the rate of 1 oz. per square yard, which is, roughly, equal to 3 cwt. per acre. A cheaper and equally effective dressing is to use basic slag and one of the meat guanos before spoken of, and this latter treatment is especially suitable to the inland links upon sandy heath soils that tend to be sour and peaty. The basic slag should be put on in winter at the rate of 6 cwt. per acre, the meat guano in February or March at the rate of 2 cwt. per acre, or ½ lb. per ten square yards. Meat guano should be selected that contains 7 or 8 percent of ammonia; those products which approximate in their composition to bone meal, with only 4 or 5 percent of ammonia, are rather too phosphatic and too little nitrogenous. The use of basic slag may at first be attended by a considerable development of fine white clover; but this is no particular detriment to the fairway of the course, and it will not persist long nor increase under the treatment. Malt culms or fish guano may take the place of the meat guano, whichever is most conveniently obtained.

On heavier soils the fairway rarely requires much manure; the problem is generally to lighten up the texture of the soil and get a better quality of herbage. For this purpose dressings of carbonate of lime are desirable, and a ton to the acre of one of the forms mentioned above should be applied in the autumn or early winter. Fertilisers will only be necessary when the land is found to be growing weeds rather than grass, through impoverishment due to too much cutting. In that case the mixture of sulphate of ammonia and superphosphate should be employed, and a dressing at the rate of 3 cwt. per acre applied in the early spring will be sufficient. Some courses on heavy land are troubled by an actual excess of clover, but nothing can prevent a rather considerable development of clover when the rains begin after a dry spell in the summer. This happens simply because the shallow-rooting clover is the first thing to feel the returning moisture, and it gets a start and goes ahead under the favourable conditions. Where clover is a nuisance, sulphate of ammonia alone may be used, applied in the spring at the rate of about 2 cwt. per acre. It will push on the grass rather rapidly, and the club's bill for mowing will be increased; but by persisting in the treatment for a year or two, the clover will be discouraged and a good quality of grass will take its place.

A few minor points remain to be discussed. Is it a good plan to rest a green and cover it with farmyard manure instead of one of the artificial dressings above mentioned? Farmyard manure does not work particularly well on the light soils we have been describing; indeed, it may become positively injurious upon peaty soils. It always promotes rather a patchy growth of grass, and it carries with it a great burden of weed seeds and very often of embryo worms which cause trouble later. One great advantage possessed by farmyard manure is the protection it affords against evaporation during droughty periods, especially in early spring, and on some of our eastern and southern coast links this mulching may be particularly valuable in saving a green that has become damaged by drought. Even then, when it is necessary to nurse a green and bring it back into good condition, it will be found better to accompany one of the artificial dressings with a coating of grass clippings cut from some of the other greens, meantime breaking the force of the wind playing over the green by surrounding it with thatched hurdles. If grass clippings are not available at the time of year, the green may be strewn with bents cut from the Marram at the side of the links, straw, or any other light rubbish. On some links a good deal of use is made of liquid manure; the sheep droppings are collected and thrown into the tank from which the water is laid on the green. This is a good practice, but, if persisted in, is apt to bring a good deal of clover, because the soluble part of the manure is rich in potash as well as in nitrogen.

In the use of artificials one or two other points should be borne in mind. They are most effective when applied early in the season, as soon as ever the grass has begun to move; they can be put on without any danger of their being washed through the soil before the plant gets hold of them. There is little need for them in autumn, and, above all, they should never be applied in hot, dry weather. Even in an east-wind spell in spring they will be found to scorch the grass and make it look very ugly, when they do not kill some of it outright. One or two minor points, not perhaps directly connected with manuring, may be mentioned here. On anything but pure sand a great deal of damage can be done, and has been done, by injudicious rolling. It is quite a mistake to suppose that grassland ought to be rolled when it is wet. To do so pastes the clay that is contained in all but the thinnest of soils, and when the surface dries it cakes and the finer grasses are choked. On many golf links immense deterioration in the quality of the grass, both on the greens and in the fairway, has set in through injudicious rolling. We may take it as an axiom that grassland on a loamy—and especially on a clayey—soil ought never to be rolled when the hand comes up wet after pressing it on the turf. Rolling is of immense value to grassland, especially on chalk soils, but the greenkeeper must catch his time as the farmer does, and roll when the surface is dry, though there is still sufficient moisture below to allow the soil to consolidate.

Chapter IV

Grasses and Grass Seeds

By Martin H. F. Sutton, F.L.S.

So many articles have appeared in recent years on the subject of the management and formation of turf that it might reasonably be supposed there is no need for further discussion of such a subject. A work like this would, however, hardly be complete without a short statement on the respective values and merits of the individual grasses which have proved useful under varying conditions.

There are, presumably, few people who still imagine that all turf is composed of one kind of grass only, which is equally suitable under every circumstance; that day has passed for ever, though my friend Mr. Colt tells me of a prominent member of an important green committee who stated his opinion that there were two kinds of grass—rye grass and some other kind! I am inclined to think that the greatly increased demand for turf of really fine texture has come about through the absolute necessity for a smooth-running surface on a putting green. Turf which, before golf became one of the national games, was considered quite good enough for a tennis court would now be utterly condemned, and the explanation lies in the fact that a small, hard, and heavy sphere like a golf ball cannot be accurately propelled along a given straight line on any turf which does not resemble in consistency the cloth of a billiard table. When once the golfer discovered that such turf was possible on a green he wanted to know why his own lawn at home was so different. How could he practise putting in his own garden on a surface consisting of plantains, daisies, buttercups, "Yorkshire fog," and rye grass grown out of character, and what was the use of his cutting a hole for the purpose under such circumstances?

Personally, I warmly welcome the change of opinion that has arisen, tardy though it has been. It has, however, had one result which, while very natural, it is none the less my duty to warn the public against. It is assumed that the beautiful velvety turf which is now so much in demand is as easy to form and as quickly brought into being as the coarse herbage which did duty for a lawn in days gone by, and it is necessary to point out that this is not Nature's way.

Every practical botanist is aware that the more highly plants are cultivated, the less seed is obtainable from such plants. The uninitiated sometimes express surprise at the high price asked for seed of the most exquisitely beautiful hot-house flowers, quite oblivious of their shy seeding characteristics. Following the same analogy, coarse species of grasses grow far more luxuriantly than the finer varieties, and turf formed from a mixture of seeds containing a large proportion of rye grass is fit for use in half, or sometimes less than half, the time required by a prescription of fine or, as I should venture to call them, up-to-date varieties. Patience is essential under such circumstances, and if undue pressure is applied to get a quick return, it will truly be a case of more haste less speed.

I have been much amused from time to time to notice the assurance of syndicates and promoters of golf courses in demanding a guarantee that the seed supplied by the successful tenderer shall produce turf fit for play in a certain number of months, and the ready way in which firms accept such terms. Given favourable climatic conditions, compliance with such a clause is a simple matter; while if the weather is adverse, no power on earth can ensure it. The usual result is litigation a few months later. Were I in a position to control the elements, I would unhesitatingly comply with such a stipulation; but since, fortunately for the rest of mankind, I have no such power, I could never, in common fairness to my correspondents, accept such a proposal. To my mind such action savours of imposture, and reminds me of the experience of an officer friend of mine who was badgered by a humbug of the begging persuasion. The latter stated that it had been revealed to him in a vision that he was Elijah, and my friend was the raven commanded to feed him! The only reply the impostor got was that my friend had "never been 'rooked' yet," and he was "not going to be 'rooked' now."

The preparation of prescriptions of grass seeds has now become a science, and the use of such mixtures varies from sowing a small plot in front of a labourer's cottage to laying down 10,000 acres of land in the Argentine or some other country in process of development. The subject is of absorbing interest, but it should only be attempted on a large scale by those who have given years of careful study to the particular characteristics of individual grasses. Unlike the drugs which constitute the ingredients of a doctor's prescription, grass glumes contain, or should contain, a living germ, and the plant resulting from the sowing of that germ will be a distinct entity with all the likes and dislikes common to the particular being, and all that is implied by that fact. While it is true that each species will respond to certain treatment, yet it is also true that within definite limits plants of the same species are capable of variation, and in studying botany this must be duly taken into account. A very interesting instance of this has been brought to my notice by a correspondent in the Riviera, who, in referring to perennial and Italian rye grass, states: "Here these give quite a different looking plant from that we are accustomed to see at home; the latter is especially deceptive in appearance."

From what has already been said, it will be clear that widely different results will be obtained from the sowing of various combinations of grass seeds. Every grass has its own idiosyncrasies, and, unlike human beings, who, though sometimes very troublesome, are amenable to argument, grasses have to be taken as they are, and treated accordingly. Some thrive in cold and exposed situations, while others would collapse under such conditions; some varieties prefer moist positions where it would be impossible for others ever to come to maturity; the majority require a firm and consolidated bed, whereas there are species which luxuriate in drifting sand.

Again, a grass which would give excellent results on one class of soil in combination with certain other grasses, in the correct proportions of each variety, will give no satisfaction whatever when those proportions are altered. That fact is not generally realised, because the majority of people who sow grass seeds do not possess the knowledge requisite to identify each plant as it comes into existence.

Speaking broadly, the stronger and coarser grasses will usually be found growing indigenously on rich or strong land, and the finer varieties on poor or light land, and it would appear consistent with the law of nature that this should be so. Moreover, a variety which in one latitude grows rank, and is classified as a weed, may in a sunnier clime be the mainstay and most valuable unit in the prescription. In many cases this is so, and the fact is of extreme importance.

Some grasses, again, possess a creeping habit, which makes them most useful ingredients in a mixture, through their power of ensuring a complete carpet of turf; others in an equal degree refuse to amalgamate, and consequently can never be sown except in combination with varieties not having this property.

The above-mentioned points will dispose of the fallacious view, still occasionally met with, that a lawn or putting green may be satisfactorily obtained from sowing one kind of grass only, which is known to suit that particular locality. If a further condemnation of such a practice is required, it is found in the fact that different varieties of grass are at their best at varying periods of the year, and consequently that, by sowing a suitably prepared mixture, turf will, under proper treatment, continue in first-class order and condition during the greater part of the twelve months. From the spring to the end of autumn there is not a month but is the season of luxuriance of one or more varieties.

I do not propose here to enter at any length into the respective merits of forming putting greens by turfing or sowing; that is dealt with elsewhere in this work. Perhaps I may, however, be permitted to point out that, while a much quicker result is obtained by turfing, it is practically an impossibility to secure turf which is free from weeds, and turf taken from one locality may, and usually does, in course of time entirely alter its character when transferred elsewhere. As an instance I may mention the famous Silloth turf, so largely used for bowling greens, which in a case under my own observation has materially changed in composition. When sowing is decided on there is this great advantage: that by a careful examination of the herbage indigenous to the immediate locality a mixture of seeds may be sown which will not only be entirely free from weed seeds, but may be guaranteed to prove suitable for the spot selected. Due consideration must, however, be given to such extremely important matters as the nature of the soil, the aspect of the land to be sown, and the average rainfall, and about each of these points a whole article could be written. To ensure, as far as may be, that the methods to be employed shall be based on correct conclusions as to existing conditions, it is an excellent practice always to make a point of obtaining a chemical analysis of the soil, so that information may be at hand as to the extent to which it is deficient in those chemical constituents necessary to the welfare of plant life. This course is the more desirable because, as has often been pointed out, when once the turf is formed, sustenance can only be applied to the roots by top dressing, which, though very efficacious, does not in any way compensate the young plants for the absence of a first-class fertiliser previous to sowing. Many an instance of weak growth of young grass plants is eventually traced to a deficiency in the soil of certain necessary constituents which are as vital to their successful development as suitable food is to the child; yet one constantly meets with people who, on the score of economy (falsely so called), refuse to go to the moderate expense entailed by properly enriching the ground. Bitterly do they regret it later, when, as is often the case, after renovating for perhaps three successive seasons, they find that the ground has once again to be entirely broken up and operations recommenced on correct principles. The idea seems to be ingrained into the minds of the uninitiated that though it is perfectly reasonable to dung ground for the use of vegetables, it is to an equal degree absurd to do so previous to sowing grass seed, and when surprise is expressed at such an attitude of mind the answer often is: “Oh! It is only grass.” The folly of such an answer is best demonstrated by two facts of extreme importance: firstly, that whereas vegetables are off the ground in two or three months at the outside, grass continues to grow, and therefore to draw nourishment from the soil throughout the whole growing period, from March until November; and, secondly, that while the kitchen garden can be dunged for each successive crop, this is out of the question in the case of grass, which is permanent.

Prescriptions of grass seeds differ in the respective proportions of each kind to the whole mixture rather than in the range of varieties used, though, as has already been demonstrated, some grasses are useful for one purpose and some for another. It is astonishing what widely diverse results will follow from the sowing of two prescriptions containing exactly the same varieties, but in different proportions. Some grasses have a masterful way of pushing to the front under almost any circumstances, and consequently should only be used in strictly limited quantities. A remarkable instance of a particularly vigorous-growing plant which, when used in mixtures, has precisely the contrary characteristic is a species of clover but little used in this country, *Trifolium pannonicum* by name. Sown alone, it produces individual plants of very robust appearance, and grows three feet in height; yet sown in a mixture, it almost invariably capitulates and soon entirely disappears.

While in the British Isles no less than 300 species of grass are to be found in the formation of golfing turf, whether through the fairway or on putting greens or tees, not more than twelve to fifteen varieties are of general use in Northern Europe, though the list may be somewhat increased when semitropical climates are included. Of this number some half-dozen are the mainstay of most mixtures, and it is of supreme importance that reliable stocks should be obtained, of proved vitality and free from weed seeds. This may seem a truism in the present day, when so much is heard of the guaranteeing of purity and seed-testing stations are established in many countries; but unfortunately the warning is all too necessary. Only those who are intimately acquainted with the handling of grass seeds have any conception of the amount of rubbish revealed by an up-to-date cleaning machine; even the expert is often unprepared for such a result. It may therefore be left to the imagination of the reader to grasp the condition of a mixture of seeds supplied by those who have no suitable facilities for cleaning, or who, having the means, do not make proper use of them.

Only quite recently there came under my notice a sample of seeds which had been sent by the secretary of an important club in the North of England with the request for a quotation for a specification that would match them; these seeds, the writer of the letter added, had been supplied by a highly respectable seed firm (mentioning the name). The mixture in general composition was quite suitable for the purpose for which it had been prepared, but it contained no less than 5 percent of weeds and dirt, and such undesirable coarse species as

Playing the 4th, Karle Kemp, North Berwick

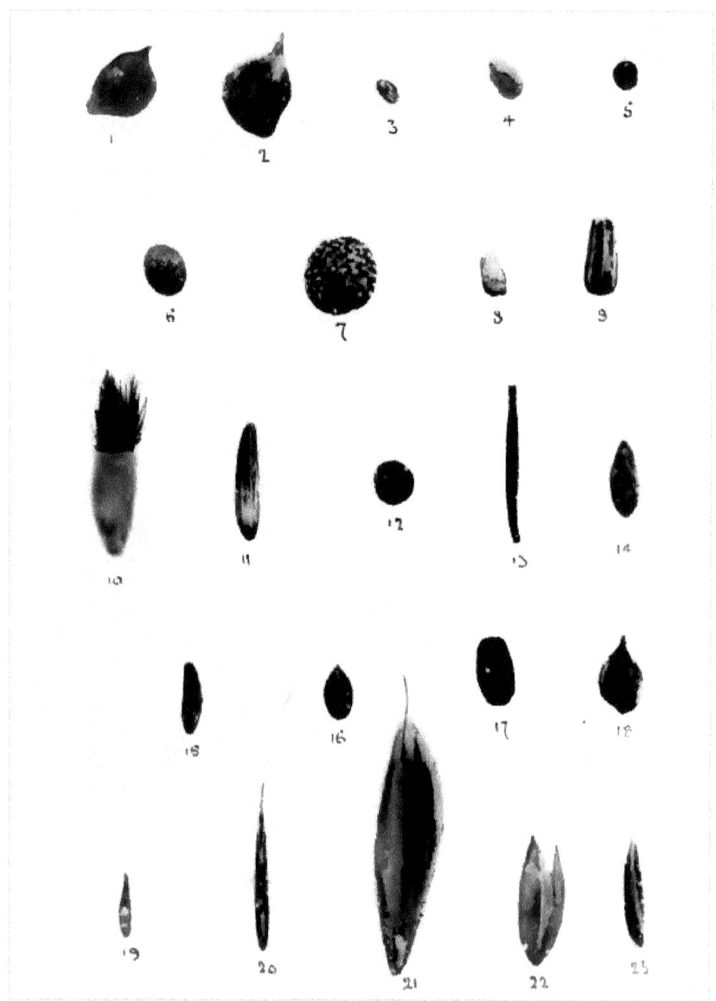

Weed seeds found in impure grass seeds

1. RANUNCULUS ACRIS (Meadow Buttercup) 2. RANUNCULUS REPENS (Creeping Buttercup)
3. CAPSELLA BURSA-PASTORIS (Shepherd's Purse) 4. VIOLA TRICOLOR (Wild Pansy)
5. STELLARIA MEDIA (Chickweed) 6 GERANIUM DISSECTUM ("Robin")
7. GALIUM APARINE (Cleavers) 8. ANTHEMIS ARVENSIS (Corn Chamomile)
9. CHRYSANTHEMUM SEGETUM (Corn Marigold) 10. CENTAUREA CYANUS (Cornflower)
11. LAPSANA COMMUNIS (Nipplewort) 12. CHENOPODIUM ALBUM (White Goosefoot)
13. LEONTODON AUTUMNALIS (Autumn Hawkbit) 14. SONCHUS OLERACEUS (Sowthistle)
15. CREPIS VIRENS (Smooth Crepis) 16. PRUNELLA VULGARIS (Selfheal)
17. PLANTAGO LANCEOLATA (Plantain) 18. RUMEX CRISPUS (Curled Dock)
19. AGROSTIS SPICA-VENTI (Silky Bent Grass) 20. FESTUCA MYURUS (Mousetail Fescue)
21. BROMUS MOLLIS (Soft Brome Grass) 22. HOLCUS LANATUS (Yorkshire Fog)
23. AIRA FLEXUOSA (Wavy Hair Grass)

Holcus lanatus, Phleum pratense, Dactylis glomerata, and *Agrostis stolonifera*. Such action is, to say the least of it, utterly inexcusable, and the result of sowing a prescription of this nature is that endless trouble is given to the greenkeeper or groundsman, as the case may be. There are plenty of indigenous weeds in every superficial foot of soil without adding to the trouble by deliberate carelessness and neglect.

But to return to my subject. Of the stronger-growing varieties there is no grass quicker in result, or more generally to be found on the fairway of the majority of courses, than perennial rye grass. It is said to have been the first grass cultivated in Europe, and was mentioned by Dr. Plot in 1677. It was used on the Chiltern Hills in Oxfordshire, and also in Berkshire, where at one time it was called "church-bent" grass. Dr. Plot, in describing its use, says: "They have lately sown ray grass to improve cold, sour, clayey weeping ground, unfit for Sanfoin." Its name "ray grass" (now more commonly called rye grass) is derived from the French word *ivraie*, meaning darnel, the common name of the noxious variety *Lolium temulentum*. Its supporters and its detractors are fairly equally divided. Some assert that there is no name bad enough for it, while others look upon it as the mainstay of every mixture. The explanation is that on certain soils it gets quite out of hand, and exhibits a tendency to coarseness which puts it out of court altogether even for the fairway. For the green it should never be used, except in climates such as the Riviera, and then only under the most exceptional circumstances. On heavier soils it is particularly valuable and is often used, owing to its remarkably quick growth, as a protector to the finer grasses, which are slow of development and less robust, though it may not be wanted as a permanent factor. I know of at least one instance where it never lasts more than a year or two, but it is regarded as invaluable for the purpose mentioned above. On the other hand, perennial rye grass is on the majority of soils one of the most durable grasses we have, and experiments at Rothamsted, extending over many years, have proved that there is nothing to touch it for longevity when sown on soils which suit it. It is undoubtedly true that it is less the fashion now than was formerly the case to include it in a mixture for the fairway, but it will always have a large number of supporters, owing to its quick growth and its comparative cheapness, compared with the finer varieties. There is this also to be remembered, that its quick development not only helps to form turf in a very short time, but also to a great degree smothers the indigenous weeds and prevents them from getting the hold which they would otherwise obtain. Again, mixtures which do not contain perennial rye grass cannot but be very expensive, and when a large acreage is to be sown this is a consideration, even in the case of the wealthiest clubs. Rye grass in southern latitudes, and especially in the Riviera, needs to be used with great discrimination. Under such circumstances it grows so quickly and luxuriantly as effectually to smother the finer grasses altogether. Sown alone, it has its uses; but where mixtures of grasses are concerned it is in the majority of cases better omitted in the Riviera. Perennial rye grass often causes annoyance, owing to the long "bents" which the plant sends up, and which defy all attempts of the machine to remove. "Bents," however, ought not, and need not, ever have been permitted to develop if the young plants had been properly topped with the scythe or mown with a high-set and sharp-bladed mower before they became too strong, and the plant should not have to bear blame which is rightly due elsewhere.

Festuca rubra (Red Fescue) is a grass of which much more will be heard during the next few years than has been the case in the past. It is the only fescue that creeps extensively, and its powers of withstanding drought and its partiality for dry climates greatly enhance its value. To the want of knowledge as to its merits on the part of those interested in the formation and care of turf I attribute the fact that the majority of dealers of seeds were long unaware of its distinction from Hard Fescue (*Festuca duriuscula*), and consequently the latter has been supplied in innumerable cases when Red Fescue has been asked for. The habits of the plants are, however, entirely distinct, as also are the purposes for which they should be used. Even at the present day Red Fescue is a grass of which it is extremely difficult to obtain clean, pure seed; when the true variety is secured it is constantly found to contain an admixture of rye grass and *Holcus lanatus* (Yorkshire Fog), the latter being a particularly pernicious weed the introduction of which on a putting green would be disastrous. There is certainly no grass of more value for general use on golf courses, and on light and sandy soils it may be employed freely in conjunction with other varieties which favour such conditions. It is specially valuable on putting greens.

Festuca rubra grows successfully even in pure sand, and a subspecies of it may be found frequently in Lincolnshire and other Eastern counties on the seashore above the high-water mark.

Festuca duriuscula (Hard Fescue) is the best-known and most extensively used of all the finer fescues, and is of a glaucous colour, quite distinct from every other grass. On all soils which are not too damp it flourishes, and is particularly hardy and vigorous. It withstands any reasonable amount of cold or drought, is the most robust of all the fescues, and may well be included in mixtures for the fairway under almost all circumstances. Owing to its hardiness and capacity for enduring constant wear and tear, it is also very useful for sowing on tees, where probably turf has to undergo more rough usage than on any other part of the course. And here, at the risk of "rushing in where angels fear to tread," I must express my surprise at the comparative neglect of the teeing grounds that is noticeable on many a course. The severe strain put upon a teeing ground through its continuous and none too gentle use would, one might have supposed, have proved its claim to special consideration. Yet on courses where the greens are kept in most excellent condition the "tees" are often rough and untidy, and sometimes do not even face correctly in the direction of the hole. I have even found tees sloping downwards, instead of being constructed on a perfect level or with a slight rise upwards—a feature appreciated by the long-handicap man, and surely excusable under certain circumstances. But that is by the way. Hard Fescue should never be sown alone; it forms plants which on occasion refuse to amalgamate one with another, and it is therefore essential that other grasses should be sown with it which will fill up the intervening spaces and so bring about a complete turf. Hard Fescue also happens to be one of the easiest grasses from which to save seed, and consequently is usually to be purchased at a lower price than any other fescue. On this account, when club secretaries fail to insist on knowing the exact composition of the mixtures they are sowing, unscrupulous dealers do not hesitate to supply a mixture containing 75 percent, or even more, of Hard Fescue, knowing that, owing to the difficulty of obtaining an analysis, there is practically no risk of detection. I would urge all purchasers of grass seeds, whether for golf courses or any other purpose, to insist on having details of every mixture supplied, and to refuse to be put off with the story of some proprietary trade secret, which is far too often made the excuse for refusing to furnish such information. The honest seedsman has nothing whatever to fear from taking his client into his confidence.

Festuca ovina (Sheep's Fescue)—This variety, though offered in almost every seedsman's list, is very little known, and there are many people who are under the impression that it is synonymous with Hard Fescue. It is exceedingly difficult to obtain true seed, owing to the fact that the harvest is generally a limited one. Were it procurable in quantity it would be far more in demand than it is, for it has much to do with the formation of the beautifully soft "Down" turf of which so much is heard nowadays, and, owing to the depth of its roots, it does not turn brown in dry weather to the same extent as other Fescues. Under normal conditions its colour is a brilliant emerald green, which delights the eye. As its name indicates, this variety is particularly popular with sheep, and its fine succulent foliage is in every way suited to their use. It has been stated, probably with considerable truth, that the fine quality of South Down mutton is largely due to the abundance of this grass on the downs on which they graze.

The Fescues are said to derive their generic name from the Celtic word *fest*, which signifies "food" or "pasturage." They are usually found in quantity on poor, sandy or peaty soil, and do not favour rich or heavy land in proportion to other stronger-growing varieties. While the question of fertilisers and artificial manures is outside the range of this article, I may point out that turf consisting chiefly of fine Fescues should never be fed with a fertiliser the least degree forcing in character, or the beautiful texture of the sward may be ruined and the Fescues give place to coarser varieties. This and kindred subjects are very fully dealt with in this work by one who is universally recognised as a leading authority on such matters.

Festuca ovina tenuifolia (Fine-leaved Sheep's Fescue) —Owing to the extremely slender nature of the blades of its foliage, this Fescue is of very great value on putting greens, and has much to do with the formation of the exquisite, fine-quality turf which is fortunately now so often to be found on first-class

10th hole, Sunningdale

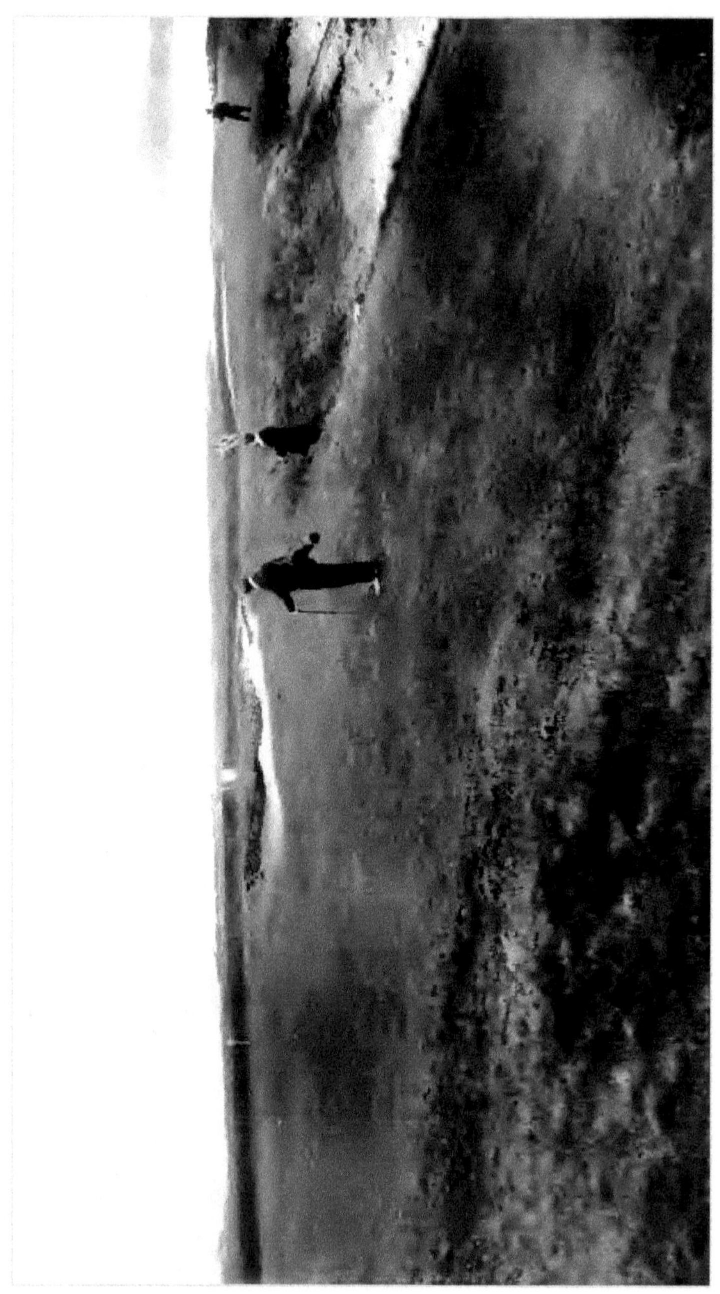

The Redan, North Berwick

courses. If the experience of an expert is needed to decide the proportions of the grasses to be used in any mixture, it is particularly so in the case of Fine-leaved Sheep's Fescue, and it is literally true to say that a slight alteration one way or the other in the quantity of this variety used to the bushel may lead to most unexpected and surprising results. That "a little knowledge is a dangerous thing" is as true now as ever it was, and a badly balanced mixture of grass seeds prescribed by an amateur with only an elementary knowledge of the subject may have, proportionately, as serious consequences as were predicted of the chemist's errand boy in the Bardell v. Pickwick trial, whose prevailing impression was that Epsom salts were oxalic acid, and syrup of senna laudanum!

Cynosurus cristatus (Crested Dog's-tail) is a deservedly popular grass which remains green in a dry spell when other varieties have lost their freshness. It is slow-growing, and does not come to perfection for two or three years after sowing. Its roots are very penetrating, and the plant, like Hard Fescue, will stand a lot of wear. While generally useful through the fairway, it is essentially a grass that is valuable for inclusion in a mixture for sowing on tees. It should, however, in my judgment, be only included in a putting green mixture under exceptional circumstances, owing to the character of its blades, which look unsightly in conjunction with the fescues and fine poas. The peculiar name of the grass is, of course, due to the flower-head, which has a distinct resemblance to a dog's tail. When allowed to grow to maturity uncut the stems are hard and unpalatable even to cattle, but are used largely for the manufacture of plait for leghorn hats and bonnets.

Agrostis vulgaris (Common Bent Grass)—This grass was long regarded as little better than a weed. Only so recently as the middle of the last century a leading botanist described it as of not sufficient importance to merit the attention of agriculturists. So far as food for stock is concerned, this is still largely true, but it is yearly growing in favour on golf courses on account of its creeping character and dwarf foliage. It is especially serviceable on dry heathlands, but should be employed with caution on heavy soils. For putting greens I should hesitate to recommend it, except where very special care is taken of the turf, as when in the least degree neglected it throws out hard spikelets running almost parallel with the turf, which are quite capable of deflecting a ball from its course, and defy the mowing machine. When given constant attention, however, it is most valuable for use in a putting green mixture where the soil is poor, and it has a marked capacity for resisting drought. I should add that it is a matter of the greatest possible difficulty to obtain pure seed, owing to the extraordinary similarity between the seed of this variety and other forms of Agrostis, some of which are rank, coarse weeds which would do untold harm to a green. Botanists are sometimes deceived even with the aid of a microscope. Quite recently I had the opportunity of examining plants grown from seed supplied under the name of *Agrostis vulgaris* by several prominent seedsmen both in Europe and in America, and was not altogether surprised to find that there were extremely few plants that were true, nearly all being specimens of one or other of the taller-growing species, utterly unsuited to form fine turf. The plant flowers very late, but is in leaf by the middle of April. In Italy and the South of France it was at one time a common practice of the poor to collect the stolons of different species of Agrostis from the roadsides and hedges and offer them for sale, done up in small bundles, as food for horses.

Poa pratensis (Smooth-stalked Meadow Grass) is one of our best-known grasses, and may be usefully employed under almost any circumstances, though, of course, in varying proportions in accordance with the conditions prevailing. It has a preference for light, dry soils, and when happily situated the plant creeps extensively. Being somewhat slow in development, it should never be sown alone; but once established it produces a large quantity of herbage early in the season, and comes to maturity about the end of June. The plant may be freely recommended not only for the fairway, but also for use on putting greens, though, owing to the width of its leaves and the great diversity in that respect between it and any of the Fescues, it is occasionally objected to—somewhat unreasonably, as I think. *Poa pratensis* is beautifully compact in habit, and with ordinary care never becomes coarse. While it is sometimes sown on heavy land, it seldom thrives under such conditions, and should therefore not form any large proportion of a mixture for land of that nature.

Poa trivialis (Rough-stalked Meadow Grass)—Unlike the foregoing, this variety revels in a damp situation, and it is consequently very useful on strong land of a clayey nature. In colour a particularly bright green, it invariably looks fresh, and has the additional advantage of flourishing under trees or in shady spots. It delights in the shelter afforded by other grasses, and so much is this the case that experiments have proved it will give double as much herbage when growing in combination with other varieties as it does when alone. It comes to maturity at the beginning of July.

Poa nemoralis (Wood Meadow Grass) is one of the most valuable permanent grasses of fine texture in cultivation. In exposed situations it grows well, but in its natural state is usually found on rich soil. For putting greens it might be used with advantage far more freely than it is. It shares with *Poa trivialis* a taste for shady situations, and is therefore specially suitable for sowing on greens which do not enjoy much sunshine. It commences to make growth very early in the spring, but does not come to maturity until the end of July or beginning of August.

While the above list comprises all the more important grasses which are in general use and suitable for golf courses, there remain one or two varieties about which a few words may be desirable.

Poa annua (Annual Meadow Grass) is usually looked upon as an exceedingly troublesome weed, and is noticeable as being the plant which infests our garden paths, and appears capable of growing everywhere and under almost all conditions. It is constantly the subject of somewhat heated correspondence, many claiming that its appearance year after year proves it to be a perennial and not an annual; it is quite correctly named, however, the explanation being that the plant is continually reseeding itself from March to October. To this fact is also due its amazing power of spreading in every direction, the seed being constantly blown about by the wind. The plant produces seed in a shorter time than any other species of grass, and it even flowers when, owing to the sterility of the soil, it cannot attain to more than an inch in height. It thrives to a remarkable degree in London squares, and one of the most interesting cases known to me of its successful predominance, to the exclusion of almost all other grasses, is in the lawns of the Temple Gardens.

While this species is the subject of much abuse, its advent is often a useful reminder to the greenkeeper that the green on which it appears needs attention. Nature abhors a vacuum, and if turf is allowed to become poor and thin for want of nourishment, plants such as *Poa annua* or moss will take the place of the finer grasses. *Poa annua*, owing to its power of resisting drought, is of considerable value in hot and dry climates, though through the difficulty of collecting seed, consequent upon the dwarf habit of the plant, it will always remain expensive. An effectual method of checking it is an application of common salt once or twice a year.

Cynodon dactylon (Creeping Dog's-tooth Grass), also known as Bermuda Grass and as the Doob Grass of India, is quite useless in Great Britain. In warm climates, however, it is largely used, and when not allowed to develop a coarse character is most serviceable where other grasses fail. Beautiful lawns are formed from it in Egypt, and turf is obtained both by sowing seed and by planting. Its remarkable success in hot climates is largely due to its curious habit of re-rooting itself at the nodules of the stems. Its roots have considerable medicinal value. In the East Indies its foliage is highly valued as food for horses. In India, on account of its wonderful power of withstanding heat and drought, it is regarded by the natives with almost superstitious reverence, as will be evinced by the following quotation taken from the fourth "Veda": "May Durva [Doob Grass] which rose from the water of life, which has a hundred roots and a hundred stems, efface a hundred of my sins, and prolong my existence on earth for a hundred years."

At the risk of wearying the reader with what is sometimes considered a dry subject, I think this article would hardly be complete without some reference to the more useful and ornamental grasses which may advantageously be sown in bunkers and for the purpose of forming floral hazards. It is a cause for real congratulation that the hideous and plain bunkers that were the fashion a few years ago are rapidly becoming a thing of the past, and every year the artificial hazards that have to be created to make a course all it should be are becoming more and more artistic and picturesque. Taking first the better known varieties:

Dactylis glomerata (Cocksfoot) certainly deserves recognition. When in flower, a fancied resemblance to fingers may be noticed in the divisions of its heads. It is decidedly ornamental, and is particularly strong and vigorous in growth on medium and strong soils, but is hardly to be recommended for light or sandy courses. It is known in America, where it originated, as "Orchard Grass," and, as that name implies, grows successfully under trees, a useful characteristic possessed by few other varieties. Though it does not flower until June, its herbage is luxuriant even in April.

Phleum pratense (Timothy or Meadow Cat's-tail)—This grass may be strongly recommended for use in bunkers on heavy or peaty land, but should not be sown on light soil. It was introduced by Timothy Hanson, to whom it owes its name, from New York and Carolina about 1780; but while American in origin, it is now widely distributed throughout this country. It is particularly hardy, and will pass quite unscathed through periods of extreme heat or cold. It grows very quickly, and is distinctly attractive when in flower.

Agrostis stolonifera (Fiorin, or Creeping Bent Grass)—Unlike *Agrostis vulgaris*, alluded to earlier in this article, this species is quite unsuited for use on greens. It is, however, a most graceful variety, and will prove a pleasing addition to the grasses usually sown for floral hazards. Its tastes are in direct opposition to *vulgaris*, for it revels in damp and undrained land, and will grow well under conditions which other grasses could not survive. It flowers about the second or third week of July.

Brachypodium sylvaticum (Slender False Brome Grass) is eminently suitable for hazard work. It grows from one to two feet high, and may be sown with safety in damp, shady situations, but it will also do well on open ground. The plant is specially useful where rabbits are a nuisance, as they will scarcely touch it, even during severe frost or snow. It is indigenous to this country, and may be sown at any altitude under 1,000 feet, above which it fails, and it comes into flower about the beginning of July.

Brachypodium pinnatum (Heath False Brome Grass)—Though a close relative of the above, *pinnatum* is distinguishable from it, owing to its more upright growth, while it possesses a creeping root, in contradistinction to the fibrous root of *sylvaticum*. It thrives on chalky soils and on heaths.

Phalaris arundinacea (Reed Canary Grass) is of a highly ornamental character, growing 2 feet high or more, according to the nature of the soil, and flowering about the second week in

July. It does best on heavy clay, and in its natural condition is to be found growing along the water's edge. It should not be sown on light land.

Hordeum pratense (Meadow Barley Grass)—While, perhaps, not so attractive as some, this variety may be usefully included amongst the list of grasses suitable for bunkers and floral hazards on account of its hardy and strictly perennial character. It is, however, not at home in sour, undrained, or very light soil, but thrives on medium land and is partial to chalk. *Hordeum pratense* resembles rye, and it has been observed with a considerable amount of truth that the term "rye grass" should be applied to this variety, and not to *Lolium perenne*, which, as already indicated, was originally known as "ray grass." *Hordeum* is, of course, the botanical name for barley, which, it is interesting to note, was cultivated by the Romans both for their horses and their armies, and the gladiators were called *Hordiarii* on account of their living on this grain.

Bromus inermis (Awnless Brome Grass)—This grass is now used to a considerable extent for binding the soil of embankments, owing to its custom of developing long underground stolons. It is quite unaffected by severe climatic conditions, and is equally insensible to heat and cold. It is a handsome variety, and is well worthy of mention.

While all the above grasses are suitable for use in floral hazards, and will greatly add to the picturesqueness of a course, it is desirable to point out that they are liable to bruising by iron play. This, however, should not, in my opinion, condemn them, and they are too good to be disqualified on that account. The following species are tougher in texture, and capable of withstanding unlimited rough usage.

Elymus arenarius (Upright Sea Lyme Grass) is a strong glaucous plant, very common on the seashore. Under analysis it has been found to contain over a third of its own weight in sugar, and for that reason has sometimes been called the sugar cane of Great Britain. It grows from 2 feet high upwards, and has been known to reach 5 feet, and it has a creeping root which makes it valuable for binding sand. In light, sandy bunkers it looks very ornamental, and will grow freely under suitable conditions; but it is essentially a seashore plant.

Ammophila arundinacea (Sea Reed, Marram, or Mat Grass), also known botanically as *Arundo arenaria*—There is no grass which possesses such remarkable powers of binding sand as this variety, and its value is such that an Act of Parliament was passed in the reign of George II for its protection, one clause of which made it penal for anyone to be in possession of a plant within eight miles of the coast. Probably there is no more likelihood at the present day of proceedings being taken under this clause than there is of the punishment of an Oxford undergraduate for playing marbles on the steps of the Sheldonian Theatre, which is contrary to the statutes of the University. Possibly some enterprising undergraduate may test this point some day, as the late Bishop Hannington is said to have tested a similarly out-of-date Oxford statute when he ran down "The High" in cap and gown pushing a wheelbarrow.

Marram grass may be successfully cultivated inland on light soils; but its home is the sand dune, where its roots become thickly matted. In countries such as Holland, where the dunes form the natural barrier against the sea, it is invaluable, and it is probable that but for this grass and *Elymus arenarius* a great part of Holland would long ago have disappeared.

Ulex Europaeus (Gorse, Furze, or Whin) is too well known to require any description. Some exponents of the game consider it a nuisance on any course, and certainly annoyance is excusable when a new half-crown ball is so effectually buried in gorse as to defy the united efforts of two caddies, one's opponent, and oneself to reveal its whereabouts. On courses such as Huntercombe, however, where it is used to separate the fairways, it teaches the player to keep straight as perhaps nothing else does, and the short but straight driver has a not unreasonable advantage over the slashing long driver, who is elsewhere apt to attribute undue importance to the length of his drive at the expense of accuracy. On the other hand, the majority of golfers today would object—and rightly so, in my judgment—to heavy banks of gorse on the line of play, even as hazards, unless by constant attention they are maintained in a sufficiently thin condition to allow of a reasonable chance of finding a ball. On a small course, the hazards of which consist entirely of whin, I knew of a boy who bought himself a new suit of clothes with the cash obtained through the sale of balls he had found in these hazards within the space of one year. Such things ought not to be.

Chapter V

Golf Architecture

By H. S. Colt

This is a somewhat dangerous subject to attempt to write about, owing to the innumerable opinions held by golfers of every degree concerning the individual merits of various courses. However, the golf course architect soon realises how impossible it is to please everyone, and sifts quickly the chaff from the wheat in the matter of suggestions appertaining to his work.

There are some opinions that I value very greatly, and if, for instance, my old friend, Mr. J. L. Low, were to criticise my work unfavourably, I should feel that there must be something wrong; but if this comes from the man who has just one idea in his head, even if he be a good player—well, then, one does not pay quite the same attention. Fashions in golf courses, as in ladies' clothes, seem to be so frequently hopelessly exaggerated. We have our latest Parisian styles, and they are adopted for every form and every contour, quite regardless of the land to be dealt with. Cross bunkers are made on a course, and they are dumped down everywhere; then wing hazards have their vogue, and we see them cut at every hole exactly opposite each other and at precisely the same distance from the tee.

Then courses are supposed to be too short, and they are at once lengthened to about four miles from tee to hole; and then we have the advocates for difficult shots, and the entrances to the greens become so small, and the bunkers so gruesome, that no one but an idiot plays for the shot. Now we have what is known as the Alpinisation of courses, and the few rough mounds which have been made for many years past develop into continuous ranges on every new course. A good idea is

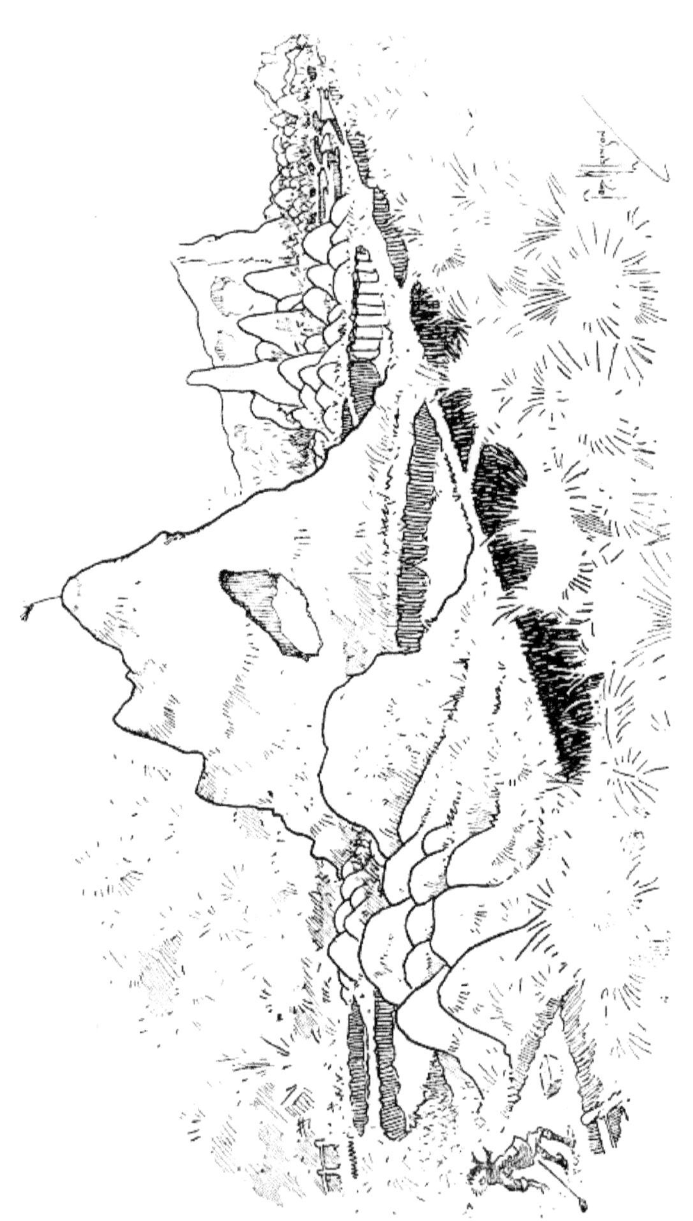

Being particularly anxious that we should have one perfect hole on our new course, we canvassed separately the opinions of six of our leading links architects as to the construction. Their ideas we adopted *in toto*, and feel that now we have at least one ideal hole!

P.S.—450 yards round the corner is the green where the real difficulties concentrate.

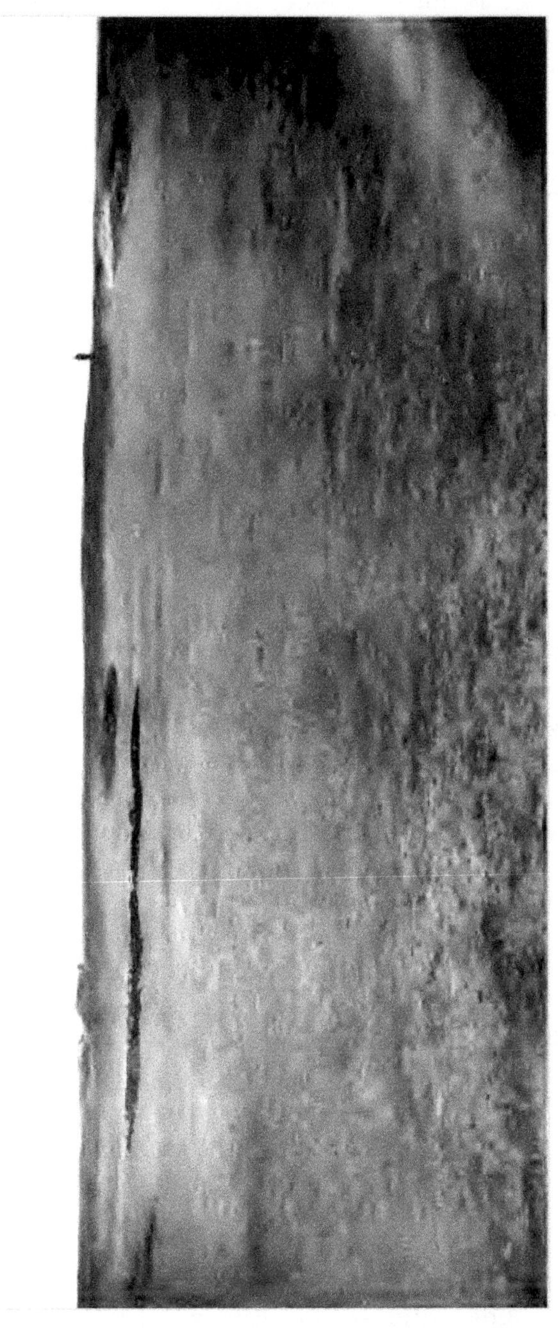

11th, Old Course, St. Andrews

worn threadbare in next to no time in golf course construction. I was asked recently to reproduce the old course at St. Andrews quite irrespective of my own want of capacity and of that of the site as well. The attempt at reproducing well-known holes with hopelessly different materials is the most futile nonsense of the lot. How often have I seen a piece of ground suitable for a good short hole spoilt by a silly attempt at reproducing the 11th hole at St. Andrews! No; I firmly believe that the only means whereby an attractive piece of ground can be turned into a satisfying golf course is to work to the natural features of the site in question. Develop them if necessary, but not too much; and if there are many nice features, leave them alone as far as possible, but utilise them to their fullest extent, and eventually there will be a chance of obtaining a course with individual character of an impressive nature.

Doubtless the first question asked is: How is it possible to do this? Do not let anyone suppose that I can personally answer this; but it is quite certain that no one can do good work in this direction unless he has plenty of opportunity to consider the subject quietly. If anyone attempts this sort of work on a bleak November day, accompanied by a large garrulous committee, each member of which has a pet theory of his own, it is also quite certain that the result will be feeble. A congenial atmosphere is necessary, and the old gentleman who desires to retail at great length every stroke played during the last round for the monthly bogey competition is enough to drive any scheme out of anyone's head. I well remember some years ago being one of such a committee, and we had a very amusing experience. A leading man on the subject was introduced for the first time to 150 acres of good golfing ground, and we all gathered round to see the golf course created instantly. It was something like following a water-diviner with his twig of hazel. Without a moment's hesitation he fixed on the first tee, and then, going away at full speed, he brought us up abruptly in a deep hollow, and a stake was set up to show the exact position of the first hole. Ground was selected for the second tee, and then we all started off again, and arrived in a panting state at a hollow deeper than the first, where another stake was set up to show the spot for the second hole. Then away again at full speed for the third hole, and so on. Towards the end we had to tack backwards and forwards half a dozen times to get in the required number of holes. The thing was done in a few hours, lunch was eaten, and the train caught, but the course, thank heavens, was never constructed! Numbers of courses have been made almost in this sort of way, and huge sums spent in trying to remodel them, the original money being lost and the finances of the club crippled thereby. From a personal point of view it is a good thing, as it means plenty of work of a remodelling nature; but it is ridiculous not to do the work properly in the first place, even if it takes more time and the expenses are very slightly increased in consequence.

My own method is first to view the land and walk over it once or twice, and inspect it very carefully, but not to lay out a single hole; then to make a second visit, having considered the scheme in the meantime, and on that occasion to settle, if possible, the framework, and take two or three days to do so, leaving the bunkering in great part for a subsequent visit. Critics may think this too elaborate and expensive; but let them remember the thousands of pounds wasted in the past, and the cost of two or three extra days is not worth consideration, especially if it is a big scheme and several thousands of pounds are to be expended upon it. Even if only a few hundreds are to be spent, it is worth while doing the work properly, and it is impossible to do this unless a considerable amount of time is given to it.

Nothing appeals to the enthusiast so much as to be taken to a large area of suitable land with the idea of making a course there; but he does not have too many chances of creating something really good, as the majority of sites are rather depressing. If the land is suitable, there is not enough of it; or if the materials be ample, they are moderate in quality. The quantity of land required depends very largely upon its shape, as if square it will be difficult to use it up satisfactorily, but a strip two hundred yards in width is easier to deal with, especially if somewhat circular.

The first thing to do is to settle upon the site for the clubhouse, and this occasionally presents great difficulty. I always favour a fine view from the club windows, and have more than once done battle over this with those favouring only the utilitarian side—such points as nearness to a railway station or very easy access; but these matters have, of course, to be considered carefully, and it is no good perching a clubhouse on a crow's nest.

If the clubhouse site is settled, it is obviously an easy matter to select the first tee; and if the tenth tee is anywhere near, it is of advantage, especially for a club to be used by business men, as there will be two starting points, and in clubs of this description, where a large number arrive about the same time, this is an important matter.

Personally, I like a fairly long, plain-sailing hole for the first one, and think that a short hole is out of place, as if it is a good one it ought to be difficult, and it seems unfair to ask much of a man who has just stepped out of a train or motor car. A couple of long holes at the commencement get the players away from the first tee, and this is desirable from a secretary's point of view, as if his members cannot start, they always become critical and impatient. After that the sequence of the holes does not matter, and what we have to look for are four or five good short holes, several good length two-shot holes, varying from an extra-long brassie shot for the second to a firm half-iron shot, one or two three-shot holes, and two or three difficult drive-and-pitch holes. A fairly equal distribution between what I have designated as good length two-shot holes and the others of all degrees seems to me about right. What we want to have is variety, gained by utilising all the best natural features of the land, and alternating the holes of various lengths. If possible, the short holes can be divided between the odd and the even numbers, so as to give the partners in a foursome a share of each. It is, moreover, advisable to play a long three-shot hole down the prevailing wind rather than against it. And let us endeavour to avoid the zigzag backwards and forwards, and also holes of a similar character to each other, so that if a stranger come to our course he may go away remembering each hole by a distinctive feature. Some courses I can never remember—you just hit the ball many times out in the same direction over similar ground, and then hit it back again; whereas on other courses there is no difficulty in remembering the various holes because of the distinctive features. I personally dislike blind shots on a course. However, it may be quite impossible to avoid one or two, but it is not necessary to select them for short holes. To hit the ball over a mountain, and then see an opponent, who is younger in years and more active in limb, climb quickly to the crest and watch one's ball gather pace and reach an unknown bunker on the blind side of the obstacle, is enough to make even the imperturbable James Braid annoyed; but, no doubt, this sort of thing does not occur to him. It would give me but little pleasure to watch Harry Vardon at his best if I could not see what was happening to the ball when it reached the ground. A really skilful player can so wonderfully control the movements of the ball after it reaches the ground. It is always entertaining to watch a great player's methods when he is approaching the hole, and quite impossible to get the same amount of pleasure when 30 feet of sand blocks the view. Golf consisting of a blind "smack" over one mountain, followed by a blind "punch" over another, gives me about as much pleasure to watch as a game of ping-pong. Good play and bad play are, moreover, equalised to some extent, as there can never be quite the same chance for the good player to show his extra skill under such conditions. But here, again, for the sake of variety, a blind tee shot may be beneficial once or twice in the round. I would always sacrifice much on this account, but not to the extent of a blind short hole. If variety be strongly developed, we also promote the best feature of the game—different classes of strokes under varying conditions. This is the real reason why golf has become so popular not only at home, but all over the world, and it is on account of this that people do not become bored with the game. So the designer of a course has one clear duty: to try to create fresh holes of interest, and not reproduce with unsuitable materials holes similar to those already in existence. Some think, no doubt, that he is quite an unnecessary, and very likely a vexatious, appendage to the game. I was rather amused to read lately, in a very popular morning paper, an article in which mention was made of a course on the West coast. The writer, after being good enough to describe its merits, ended up his article devoutly thankful that no golf course architect had been allowed to meddle with it. The reader can guess at the source of my amusement.

It is impossible to give any definite rules on laying out a course, or to state what length it should be, as everything must depend upon the nature of the materials in each individual case. Anything round about 6,000 yards seems to be long enough, even with the new-fashioned ball. It is obvious that there are many bad long courses and many very good short courses, and length has very little to do with merit.

There is, however, one great feature that appeals to me—the elasticity of a course; and in designing the framework it is better to walk forward to the next teeing ground, and not to retrace one's steps after playing a hole. This, no doubt, is not by any means always advisable, as a good natural feature may be lost for the next tee shot; but it gives a better chance of making "back" teeing grounds to be used under special conditions. There is no doubt that a series of tees, whereby the length of a hole can be altered with varying conditions, is an advantage. If we take a new course, for instance, the run of the ball will increase with the age of the links, as the surface of the ground becomes firmer with play. The distance of a tee shot will also vary enormously in summer and winter. There were several cases of drives of about 350 yards during the summer of 1911 with the new heavy rubber-cored balls, which in summer now alter so largely the length of a course, so far as the player is concerned. Two or three years ago it was thought that a hole of about 400 yards was one which required two full shots to reach the green. The 18th hole at Sunningdale is now of nearly that length, and during the drought of the year just mentioned Jack White drove this hole from the tee on more than one occasion. So that at the holes where, under normal conditions, there is no long carry off the tee it will be advantageous to be able to obtain more length by using a back tee to suit the varying conditions of the surface of the ground, and also possibly the wind. It will be easier to do this if, after playing a hole, we usually walk forward to the next tee; but at the holes where there is already a long carry from the ordinary tee it is obviously impossible to arrange for much extra length, and when cross hazards are made for compulsory carries in playing the second shots these are the occasions for their use. The length of the drive is no doubt sacrificed, as under abnormal conditions a long hitter will be able to reach the subsequent cross hazard. He must play short, and if he is so foolish as not to do so, he probably gains intense satisfaction by telling as many of his fellow members as will listen to him the details of his great feat; while if he is not a member of the green committee, that body is no doubt referred to in uncomplimentary terms. He is satisfied, and the man who plays with judgment is satisfied, as

4th hole, Sunningdale

Good type of bunker

he has a more amusing second shot to play by reason of his self-denial on the tee. If, however, there were many examples of this class of hole on the links, long driving would be at a discount; but two or three holes of this description add to the interest of the game, and we cannot afford to sacrifice everything to the length of the tee shot. The new ball, and very likely a little more experience, have made me modify my opinions about the compulsory carry for the second shot, of which, within proper limits, the Editor of *Golf Illustrated* has always been a strong supporter.

In making the different teeing grounds it will be possible to gain a little extra variety by playing the tee shot at different angles to the course; thus a teeing ground made at some thirty yards or so to the right or left of the one in front will very likely create additional interest in the round, and be better than one made exactly behind it.

Some few years ago it was a very common idea that the first-class player was the only person to be considered when the course was laid out. Considering how few they are in number, it often strikes one how extraordinarily successful they were in getting their way. But recently the vast number of those in receipt of odds have become more alive to the possession of their power. They have even become infected by the present unrest in the labour market, and during a recent railway strike the members of a club were known to rise in a body and insist upon the restitution of a certain hole, which they considered had been unjustly taken away from them. Courses have no doubt been getting more and more difficult for the average player. His golf has in some cases been a dismal progress from the rough to a bunker, and from a bunker to the rough, hole after hole. He has very likely chosen a pleasant spring day for a little relaxation and pleasure, and returns to his home at night in a jaded and almost hopeless frame of mind. It is by no means impossible to give a weak player every opportunity of enjoying the game within his powers, and at the same time to provide a test of golf for Harry Vardon or James Braid at his very best. To do this, the designer of a course should start off on his work in a sympathetic frame of mind for the weak, and at the same time be as severe as he likes with the first-class player. The more frequently he stamps on the mediocre shot of the latter, so much the better, provided that he does not become vindictive.

I will attempt to show how this can be done. Let us start with the tee shots. It is certainly amusing to have a fair number of carries from the teeing grounds; but if these are to be of any use as a test of length to the first-class driver, they are certain to be impossible to the short player. Therefore if we want to have a carry of say, 165 yards or more, let us provide a path of safety, whilst giving advantage in the subsequent play of the hole to the player who accomplishes the test provided. The 3rd hole at Sunningdale is an example of this.

Then, again, let us take the case of lateral hazards. These can be made at such a distance from the tee that the weak player very seldom reaches them.

Or take the instance of a central hazard with a path on either side. This class of bunker is always open to criticism from the man who hits a long, straight shot down the centre of the course, without having sufficient intelligence in his head to know that the proper line is to the left or to the right, as the case may be, and that if he takes the wrong line, he deserves no sympathy. Well, in the case of such a hazard the weak player can be kept out of it by placing it beyond the limits of his drive; in fact, in designing the bunkering of a course the object should be to catch the bad or mediocre shot of the good player and punish the long-handicap man for bad strokes less than the former. Give the short player as much pleasure as you can by providing short carries off the tee (almost negligible quantities for the good player); he always appreciates them, and he is sure to find quite enough difficulty in the remainder of the course on his own account. The giver of odds has, as a rule, a big advantage when playing a match on the handicap points, and we do not want to accentuate this by giving the receiver of odds too much to do on his way round the course.

There is one class of hazard which has appealed to me very greatly for the last three or four years—the diagonal hazard. We do not want this, however, overdone and to see it everywhere, whatever the nature of the ground. But if the latter is suitable, it provides sport for everyone, and the subsequent scheme of a hole can give advantage to the one who bites off the biggest slice of the hazard. The 5th hole at Swinley Forest, and also the 5th hole at Sunningdale, especially with the green now extended to the right, are examples.

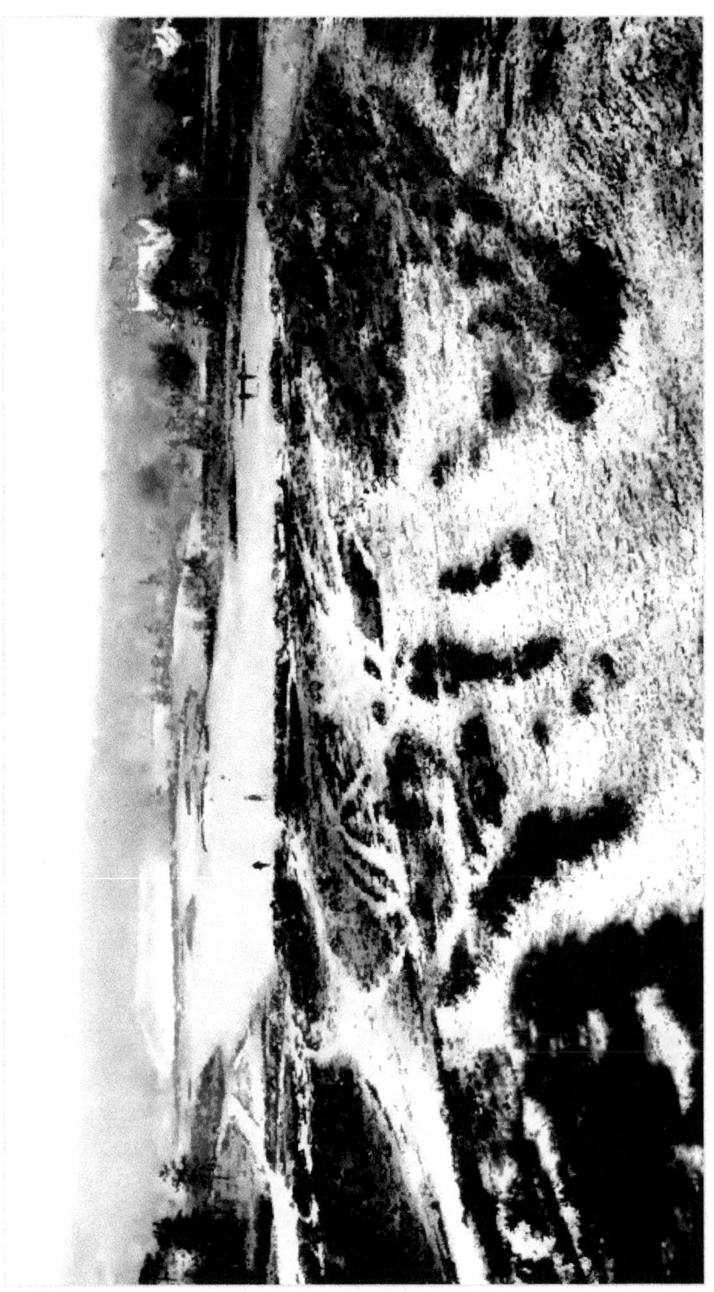

5th hole, Sunningdale

5th hole, Swinley Forest

A test of accuracy must also be provided for tee shots, and the player learn to take a line, and not just blaze away at right angles to the teeing ground. All who know the old course at St. Andrews will realise what I am attempting to explain, as their caddies have many a time told them to play on the College Church steeple or other well-known landmarks; indeed, a friend of mine even carries this to such an extreme that he told me on one occasion that, in playing the last tee shot of the round, he framed on the "D" in the words "GRAND HOTEL" displayed in large letters on the building behind the 18th green. I am not quite sure whether that shot finished on the "H" or in the area steps of the houses on the right. In providing this test for accurate driving a good sprinkling of lateral hazards is necessary. Heather is useful in this direction, and also long grass, but the latter should not take the form of the meadow just ready for the hay-cutting machine. A hayfield and golf never seem to me to go well together. The rough, sandy hummocks of a seaside links prove excellent side hazards. Then, again, the central bunker in the course itself forces a player to try to place his ball in a desired area. This placing of the tee shot, if not overdone, is one of the best features of modern golf course construction work; and it can also be easily enforced by the hazards near the green, so that they govern the tee shot even if there be no bunkers for that stroke.

A dogleg hole, like the first one at Hoylake, is to me one of the finest for an accurate test of the game. The player who can place his tee shot just past the corner of the dyke gains a big advantage there. And, again, in the old days at St. Andrews, before the rubber-cored ball was introduced, the man who could place his tee shot at the 17th hole between the corner of the wall and the bunker on the left was in a very enviable position compared with an opponent who had driven wide to the left.

It is now a case of reverting occasionally to a class of hole which used to exist when golf courses had not been almost reduced to standardisation. I refer to the occasion when a player would take a short club off the tee so as to arrive at a spot from which a long, full second shot could be played with more advantage than by reversing the order of strokes. Such a scheme will appeal to those who favour not only straight hitting off the tee, but also the placing of the tee shot in the correct position so far as length is concerned. We must not have many of these tee shots, as otherwise a premium is likely to be placed on short driving. Ground should be selected for this sort of hole, and also for a dogleg hole, which presents some natural features insisting upon or emphasising the class of shot which we are trying to develop; otherwise the effect will be laboured and artificial.

Let us now consider the approach shots on a course, whether they be a short "pitch" with a mashie or a full shot with a brassie—in fact, all strokes when the putting green can be reached. Hazards which would be perfectly fair for a short "run up" may be manifestly absurd for a full shot, as the greater the distance to be covered, the more latitude there must be for error. This creates the difficulty in designing interesting approach play for all classes of players, as all sorts of problems arise out of it. If a bunker be made at one spot for the long driver, it will be very likely unfair for the short player, and vice versa. One or two suggestions have been made previously on this point, when considering the tee shot, which may be useful now. There must always be a certain amount of conflict between the various classes of players. In the one case the ripe veteran must be occasionally sacrificed, and told that when the ground is soft and the wind in his teeth he must carry 300 yards or so in two shots or play short; and, on the other hand, the committee may occasionally have no pity for the slashing young player of twenty or so, and provide him with a pitfall when he hits an extra long one under rather abnormal conditions. We have to accept this if we are to have interesting approach play for the vast majority of players under normal conditions.

The hazards applicable for the tee shot will be suitable for the full shot played in approaching the green, and one or two cross hazards giving a long carry will be acceptable to most people. No doubt at times it will mean playing short, and thus the benefit of an extra well-hit drive will be lost, but one or two instances—I would not want more, personally—of this class of stroke are advisable. It is not everyone who can pick up a close-lying ball from hard ground with a brassie and lash it over a big bunker.

If we are to have wing bunkers near the green, the antithesis of the foregoing, we can make the passage between narrower than for the drive, as a man should have more confidence in playing his second shot than his first. We do not, however, want to see them cut exactly opposite each other and at right angles to the course.

Now we come to the class of full approach shot which always appeals to me, one which is vitally affected by the line taken from the tee. The 10th hole at Sunningdale is a good instance of this. The bunker near the green is close to the hole, but, as the ground between rises, a long second shot is pulled up in time. To see that hole played well is to me always a treat, especially if the player knows on the tee that he cannot carry this bunker with his second stroke. He has to place his tee shot to the right, and then just shave past the bunker on the left with his second, and if the hole is cut on the upper portion of the regular green, just a shade of pull is an advantage. If he fears disaster and wants safety, he can obtain it at the expense of having a long "run up" to lay dead for a "4." A hole like that is perfectly fair for everyone—the short, the medium, and the long—and gives most excellent sport for all, besides being, under ordinary conditions, a really fine test of the game. It provides the very long carry for the man of great power, it furnishes the skilful and medium-length player with a chance of playing an exceptionally good one, and it constantly supplies a short pitch for all those who fail to reach the green in two shots, and also a fair amount of niblick work. The 4th hole at Sandwich is another instance of a grand hole of the same type, although now possibly a little on the short side with the new balls. It required, at any rate, the same placing to the right of the tee shot to avoid the deep ravine on the left near the green. The drive is governed by the difficulties provided for the approach—the two hang together—as the player, when he stands on the teeing ground, is even then compelled to consider his second stroke. We need several holes of this description in our course. If anyone has to depend upon skill and judgment as against power alone, certainly penalise him if he fails to place his shot accurately. By all means give such a one an impossible carry; trap him in any way you like, and give him no quarter. But if he offend not, let us provide him in the general course of events with something possible and interesting, and not have only one rejoinder to his protest—"You can play short."

As the central and diagonal hazards have been dealt with already, we will now consider approach shots of shorter range

1st green, Hoylake

4th, Sandwich

4th, Sandwich

than the full shot. Many think that the golfer who would be well equipped in the matter of approach should be able to play three classes of strokes for such distances. He must be able to pitch high and stop quickly, to "pitch and run," and to "run up," and thus the ground is covered in three distinct ways.

It is very pleasant to watch perfect driving, and many a time—some years ago now—I thought that the driving of Douglas Rolland, especially against a strong wind, was the thing to be most envied in a game of golf. The low ball, even in the days of the "gutty," or, still farther back, the "Eclipse," used to go off the face of his club at a tremendous pace, gradually rise, but never tower, and when it reached the ground there was always plenty of life in it. How, when a boy, I envied his driving, and also his 44 inches of chest! And I well remember his favourite remark when he hit an extra good one; it was always the same—"Awa' she sails with dashing spray!" Many a round have I enjoyed in his company at Malvern, then Limpsfield, and afterwards at Rye. The last time I saw him was at Bishop's Stortford, and I do not know where he is now; but I have no doubt that, wherever it be, they will like him—I had almost said love him—as much as I did when a boy.

But if driving appeals to the boy, scientific approach play appeals to the man. And the golfer who has played some years, while no doubt admiring long and accurate hitting, probably appreciates even more the extraordinary command over the ball of such a master as Mr. J. L. Laidlay or Mr. Alan MacFie when at his best. Every stroke was individually considered, and played in neat and perfect style. When I watched them with envious eyes it was not their habit to take enormous blocks of turf with every shot, as is now so often done, to the disgust of greenkeepers. Their caddies would never dream of always dragging out of the bag the mashie just because the ball could be made to reach the hole with such a weapon. There might be a low hummock in the way at the start, and then a level run up to the hole of 50 or 60 yards; or there might be a plateau green of narrow dimensions. Would they use the mashie under these circumstances? Certainly not. They had the command of an infinite variety of shots, and would select the right one.

Now consider the firm half-shot of such players as Bob Martin with his cleek or Andrew Kirkaldy and J. H. Taylor with

Fairway from Point Garry, North Berwick

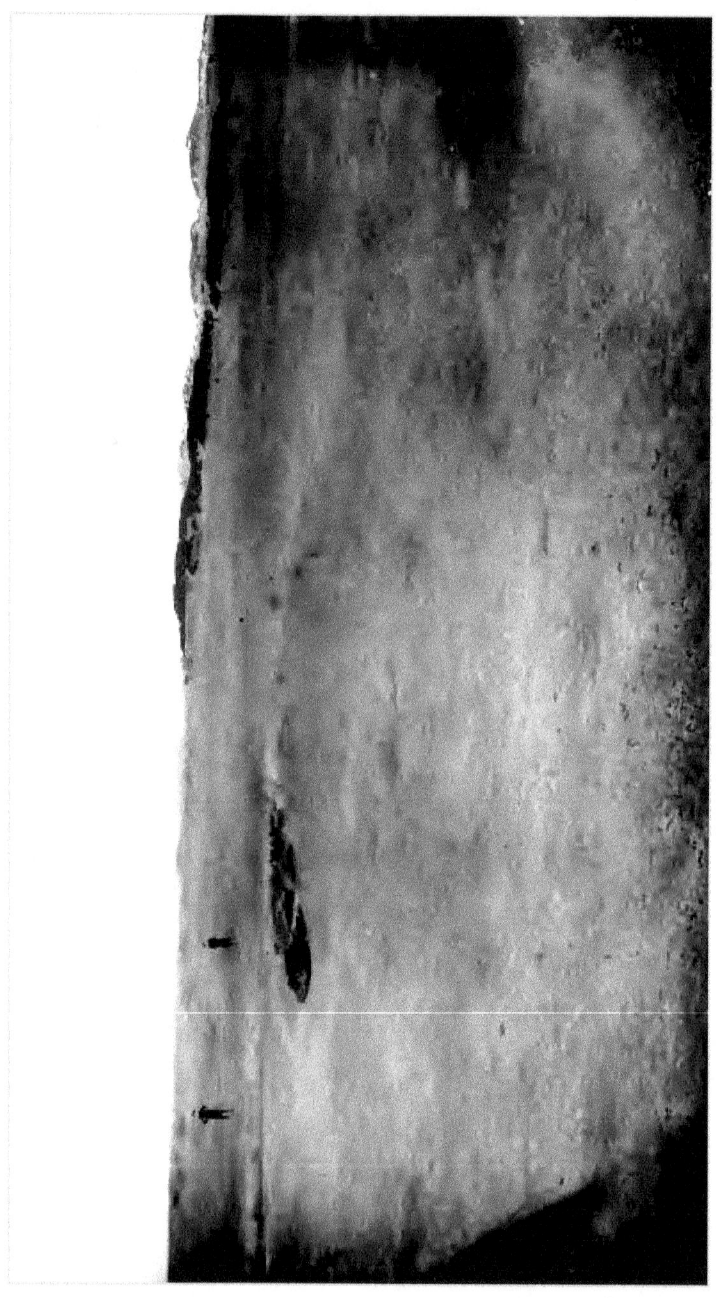

12th, Old Course, St. Andrews

their driving mashies, played with but little effort and very likely in the teeth of a strong wind. And if we are ambitious in trying to provide opportunities for testing the abilities of the real artist in approach play—and there are few more interesting things in golf than such an attempt—we shall probably find that we need further materials than bunkers and hazards of the ordinary description. If we had to depend alone upon them, the course would be either too easy for the championship player or too hard for the ordinary one. There are two classes of difficulties which are most useful for our purpose—plateau greens and "hummocky" ground. The vast majority of links need both badly. A narrow plateau for a green, or a few hummocks in front of one, will very likely cause just as much trouble and amusement to a player as a gaping chasm stretching right across the course. Without doubt, we want bunkers to pitch over; but, for the reasons previously mentioned, we cannot rely entirely upon them for creating interesting and testing approach play.

As an instance of a good plateau green, take the 12th hole at St. Andrews. There is, certainly, the small pot bunker some 50 yards or so in front of the green, but that is never the real difficulty in getting close to the pin. It is the narrow plateau and the two shoulders on each side, more particularly that on the left. The man who can only play the high pitching shot with his mashie has not much chance of a putt for a "3" here. Or for a longer approach shot, take the 16th hole on the same course, and watch Andrew Kirkaldy play it, and we shall most probably see him use a straight-faced iron club with a satisfactory result. And, again, as an instance of a hummock, let us take the 4th hole on the same course. Have we not all been bothered by it on innumerable occasions? It has proved of just as much value for the purposes of a hazard to make us try to play the right class of shot as the deepest bunker in existence.

Then, again, the turf hollow, with a "draw" into it, practically forming a portion of the putting green itself, will also help us in our endeavour to extract the very best from the champion himself. At the same time these difficulties do not call for the sacrifice of those of humbler merit. They are all certainly obstacles in their path, but the long-handicap player probably derives just as much pleasure from them as the scratch man, and this cannot be said of the ordinary type of sand bunkers. The good player can almost invariably extricate his ball from the latter with comparative ease, whereas the bad player finds them fearfully retentive.

For another purpose undulations and hummocks are of great value "through the green," as they provide difficult stances and lies, without which no golf course can be said to be quite perfect. I well remember an argument upon this point which I had some little time back at Sunningdale. The course was looking its best, having been recently cut, and the turf was even and smooth. Although when adverse criticism occurs a secretary is always liable to take the bait, yet when there is by chance fulsome praise he is just as liable to object. And when someone came up to me and admired the state of the green, out of sheer contrariness I objected, and said that the lies were getting much too good. My friend would not agree on the ground that if a good shot had been made, the player was entitled to the best of everything. But surely this can be overdone, as what we want to do, amongst other things, is to extract the very best golf from a man, and nothing does this so much as difficult lies and difficult stances. After playing over links where you never get them, it is very hard to pick up a ball from a badly hanging lie, and it needs a lot of practice and skill to play the stroke successfully. This is generally the weakness of inland courses, and where they have been ploughed up and sown with seed the surface has in the past been usually levelled at the same time, and a number of small interesting details removed.

The high pitch shot must not be left out of consideration, as we want as many of them as possible in the course; and not only the pitch shot with a mashie, but also an instance here and there of the high stopping shot with the mid-spoon. In fact, we want examples of every class and description of stroke to be played at some time or another during the round.

I have attempted to show that we can have great variety in the character of the difficulties provided for the delectation of the golfer, and if we go one step further, we can have variety in each class of hazard. The shape and nature of bunkers can be varied with immense advantage. How often do we see a delightful landscape spoilt by the creation of a number of symmetrical pots, or banks, or humps, made apparently at so much a dozen! And this landscape might have been improved, and made still more pleasing to the eye, by planting judiciously off the course irregular clumps of whins, or broom, or rough grasses, or possibly small birch trees and Scotch firs. If we have to make bunkers—and no doubt they will be necessary—we can in great measure conceal their artificiality, and in any event we need not make them of a certain stereotyped pattern. Some can be sunk without banks; some can have rough banks added to them; some can be sand and some rough grass; some can be in the nature of rough, irregular, wide grass ditches, and so on. If they are sunk, then a little treatment of the ground prior to their commencement will be a help in our attempt to remove the stain of artificiality. The ground can be gradually sloped down to the proposed level of the bottom of the hazard. A small bunker with a draw into it is often more serviceable than a large sandy waste. But wherever possible let us take advantage of a rise in the ground for a bank or of a hollow for a pot. Nature will often provide us with a small feature which will work in successfully with the scheme for a good hole.

Further, the margins of the course can in many cases be allowed to provide in great measure the difficulties for the round. If we have all our margins cut so as to give the impression of the use of the measuring rod and garden line, we shall have a course which will satisfy only the strictly golfing portion of a man's nature, and deprive him of considerable pleasure from playing the game amidst pleasing surroundings. The margins of the course can be made so as to form a bay here and a promontory there, and these will be of use as difficulties in the play of the various holes.

It is a great pleasure to some of us to break up the horrible regularity so often met with on inland links.

Putting greens are dealt with in another chapter, but nothing is said of the choice of their sites. Personally, I like to select a ridge or a low plateau in preference to a hollow. The green is obviously more visible to the player, which is a feature after which I strive. And if we can select a wide hog's-back for the purpose, we shall not need much, if any, artificial help in the nature of bunkers. Still I would not by any means wish to eliminate altogether the punch-bowl green from a course, as, although weak from the point of view of a test of skill, it is delightful in other respects. Eighteen flat greens are to me an abomination, and the pleasantly undulating green which provides "possible" putting even in a dry summer is far preferable.

On the other hand, two or three examples of the flat green are an advantage.

In conclusion, I can say that I have made no attempt to prescribe for the size of greens or tees, for the width or length of the various holes, for the depth or shape of the bunkers, as it is my firm conviction that the less said on these subjects the better. I have met with so many "thirty by thirties" in putting greens, "ten by tens" in tees, and so much similarity in bunkers, that I am sick to death of them. Immediately we attempt to standardise sizes, shapes, and distances we lose more than half the pleasure of the game. Too much stress cannot be laid upon the necessity of seeing and using the natural features present on each course to the fullest possible extent. It is only by doing this and selecting them judiciously for their special purposes that we can arrive at the success at which we aim. We must seize upon them with a grasping hand, and if possible not let one of them escape us. If perchance they be numerous and varied in character, then we shall have an opportunity of constructing a course which will give a real and genuine pleasure to all to play over, whatever their skill in the game may be.

Chapter VI

The Influence of Courses upon Players' Style

By Bernard Darwin

Long before the time when the wooden putter was scornfully christened by golfers from other courses the "Musselburgh iron," it may be presumed that different links regularly turned out different schools of players. Even now, when golfers stay so much less at home and have so many more courses to play upon, they are apt to bear the hallmark of their native course, it may be merely in some mannerism or trick of style, it may be in their whole method of play. These characteristic styles that belong to particular courses cannot, it is true, be wholly attributed to the respective natures of the courses themselves, because imitation of some venerable model plays a large part in the education of golfing youth. For example, we go to Hoylake and see a young gentleman addressing the ball with the right foot well advanced, the club sunk home in a determined grasp of the right fist, the right forefinger playing idly about as if its owner had no use for it. We further observe, perhaps, that he wears stockings with red tops to them, and walks with a rather curious gait, the knees bent and the body tilted well forward. We are not to jump at the hasty conclusion that all these characteristics have been produced by some unique quality of the Cheshire course. The explanation of these phenomena is simply that this young gentleman very properly regards Mr. John Ball as the greatest man in the world. The fact that the young North Berwick golfer takes a wide stance, and that his legs look as rigid as if they were made of iron, only shows that he holds a similar and equally justifiable opinion of Mr. Laidlay. Did not Sir Walter Simpson write of him years ago that "his

17th and 18th, St. Andrews

13th, The Pit, North Berwick

wretched imitators swarm on every links in the Lothians"? Finally, the loose and slashing style of St. Andrews must not be altogether set down to the wide nature of the course and the comparative immunity from trouble often granted to the wildest shots. That glorious free swing, with its delicious swagger, must, in a measure at least, be traceable to some departed genius who lived in the days when the whins had not yet been hacked off the face of the earth, and an erratic shot meant a painful and prickly doom.

At the same time, though imitations may account for much, and especially for superficial mannerisms, the nature of the home green must—and does—have a great deal to do with the foundation of a player's game. As long as there are that horrible steep bank on one side and the rushes and ditch on the other, as we steer our devious way to the 3rd hole at Hoylake, the Royal Liverpool Golf Club is very unlikely to produce a race of crooked drivers. Look again at the masters of mashie play that have come from North Berwick—Mr. Laidlay, Mr. Maxwell, Whitecross, Ben Sayers, the Grants, and many others. It was the old and short course that was no doubt *par excellence* the school for adroit little pitches; but the tradition of deft pitching, and in a great degree the necessity for it, survive in the present and extended courses.

Golfing architecture as a regular art or science, whichever it may be, is still so comparatively new that the many fine courses that have been made—if one may say so without offence—artificially are still too young to have produced golfing schools. Moreover, it so happens that on most of the best of these modern inland courses, which have given the architect his great opportunity, small boys are not often to be seen—are not, maybe, particularly encouraged to be seen. For both these reasons we have still to look rather at the players who learned their game on older courses—courses laid out by nature or by man more or less haphazard—in order to come to any general conclusions as to the effect of the course upon the player's game. In doing so, one is somewhat painfully conscious of the obvious pitfalls. First there is the danger of over-refinement and of attributing to a course some peculiarity which is in reality a part of the player's native genius, and would have found expression in any surroundings. Secondly, whatever rules one may propound, it is tolerably certain that there will be many exceptions to them.

I can, for example, think of a most noteworthy exception to the first rule that I very tentatively lay down—namely, that it is the long course that produces the long driver. The exception is Mr. Abe Mitchell, who is perhaps the longest driver in the world; he is, at any rate, quite as long as anyone save the tremendous Frenchman Dauge, who, according to Braid's own modest account of the matter, can hit as far with a cleek as he (Braid) can hit with a driver. Now, Mr. Mitchell learned his golf entirely at Ashdown Forest, a course particularly charming, but not particularly long. In one sense it is the very worst of courses for a mighty driver, because the man who hits the ball a long way will hardly ever be on the course at all. Belts of heather run across the fairway; and, while the modestly hit ball lies short in safety, the long ball almost always reaches the rough.

However, in spite of this outstanding exception, it may be laid down generally that length of course makes for length of hitting. Nearly every golfer must at some time or other have experienced the sensation of visiting a big seaside course after playing for some while upon a small inland one. He will remember how the big carries and the long holes have pulled him out, till he has found himself hitting farther, not because he is noticeably hitting more cleanly, but just because he has the incentive. This was, to be sure, a much more familiar experience in the days of the gutty ball. Now with the heavy little rubber-cored ball there is hardly such a thing as a very long carry; certainly there is no course that demands the continuous length of carry from the tee that Sandwich once did, and long holes are not relatively so long as they used to be. The sensation, however, may still be felt, though not so acutely as of old. It is not that long driving does not pay on a short course. In one sense it pays even more on a short course than on a long one. The man who can drive far enough to give himself a series of quite short pitches for his second shots scores enormously over an opponent who is constantly approaching with a long iron shot; the longer hitter gets, or ought to get, such a steady string of easy fours as to break down his adversary who is always putting to save his life. But though it is infinitely profitable to drive far, the profit is not such an obvious one; there is no absolute need to hit a long ball in order to reach the green in the right number of strokes. The young golfer does not, as a rule, go out of his way to think, and it is sheer hard necessity that is his best and most effective teacher.

That which surely must have a great effect on the driving of a still unformed player—a greater effect even than the length of the hole he is playing—is the number of hazards into which he may possibly get with each one of his tee shots. There has been a great disposition in modern times—and on the whole a very proper disposition—to make the player "place" his tee shot and to be terribly down on the cheerful slasher who is content to hit his ball somewhere in the direction of the hole. "Bunkers should more perfectly abound," said Mr. John Low, and his disciples have seen to it that they do abound. The result has been some admirable holes and tee shots, the mere prospect of which makes one shiver in one's shoes upon the tee; but it is possible to have too much of a good thing. I am personally a great admirer of the tee shot to the 4th hole at Woking, where one has either to hit a most prodigious carrying shot or else lay down the ball with the nicest accuracy between a railway line and a bunker, which is exactly in the middle of the fairway. In this eulogy all will not concur, and I believe Mr. Colt, for one, does not agree with me; but assuming for a moment that I am justified in admiring this hole, I am much more justified in saying that several holes of that character, coming one upon the top of the other, would be more than any reasonable golfer could stand. Certainly a course that had many such holes would be a very bad training ground for a young golfer. It would cramp him hopelessly, so that he would never learn to hit out freely. The one thing that anyone who wants to be a really good driver must learn is to swing his club with a good measure of freedom, without which, indeed, he will hardly swing it truly. To advocate freedom is not at all to advocate slogging, but no one likes to see a young golfer taking exaggerated pains to be accurate. It is also, of course, exceedingly bad for him to have a wide, open prairie into which he may hit with perfect impunity. What is good for him is almost invariably to have heather or rough ground to the right and left of the fairway, so that a really serious slice or hook shall surely be punished. It is not good for him, I fancy, to have too many pot bunkers dotted here and there on the fairway, with the result that he goes constantly in dread of his life. The pot bunkers—in moderation—are good fun for us who are past the educational stage, and have reluctantly abandoned hope of improvement this side of the Styx, but I do not believe they are very good for the young.

Needless to say, it is easily possible to err in the direction of too much room. St. Andrews, regarded as a training ground for driving, almost certainly does so err. There are plenty of bunkers, very nearly on the line to the hole, which have to be avoided with meticulous accuracy, aided in a stranger's case by some good fortune. On the other hand, the most infamously crooked shots may go for a whole round practically unpunished. As a result of this, St. Andrews turns out generation after generation of fine, free, dashing hitters. Possibly also as a result, though it produces many good players, it seems that none of them nowadays is possessed of quite that unswerving accuracy which is almost essential in the highest walks of golf today.

I am inclined to think that inland courses will give us the best drivers of the future just because of those unending lines of heather on either side of the course, which never encourage the really wild hitter in his evil ways. At least I should be very strongly inclined to this opinion were it not for an educational influence which is wholly beyond the control of the most powerful architect—namely, the wind. A wind is roaring in my chimney as I write. If I went out to the nearest suburban course, it would doubtless make me slice horribly; but how much louder it would roar, how much worse would be my slice, if I went by the ocean wave and could see the bents all heeling over in one fatal direction and luring me to my doom! There is no breeze like a sea breeze, and, important as it is in teaching a player to drive, to keep his body rigidly still, to hit now high and now low, it is probably still more important in respect to iron play. No inland course, I fancy, however cunningly made, will produce quite so sturdy, and at the same time so accomplished, a race of iron players as do the seaside ones.

Yet what extraordinary strides the inland architects have made in the direction of compelling us to acquire some variety of iron shots! How distant appears the time when only one stroke was necessary—a pitch with a mashie over a rampart placed at just such a distance from the green as to have the absolute minimum of effect! A few years ago a purely inland-bred golfer, who might be a quite effective player on his own course, had comparatively little idea of playing any running shot; when he was confronted with a plateau and a steep bank, such as are to be found at St. Andrews or at the 18th hole at Deal, he was completely at a loss. If he is so today, he has no excuse for his deficiencies. Plateaux abound on all sides; there are at least two copies in existence at Pandy and Musselburgh, one at Huntercombe and two others at Worplesdon. Moreover, there are innumerable holes where, granted a tee shot hit to the right place, the best and easiest method of approach is a straight running shot.

Thus the young inland golfer ought now to be able to acquire some variety of strokes with his irons. There does, however, appear to me to be one danger—namely, that he will stereotype the running-up or pitch-and-run shot, while losing, or rather never acquiring, the art of really skilful pitching. It is not by any means altogether due to the trend of golfing architecture, but the fact remains that the golfer of today does not learn so thoroughly as did his predecessors the art of playing approach shots with cut. For this there must be various and complex reasons, which it is hard to disentangle. One of them may be the rubber-cored ball. It was possible with a skilful stroke to make the gutty ball rise more abruptly than the rubber core; but when it is merely a matter of getting the ball into the air somehow, then the rubber core is up to a point the easier to play with, and the more flattering to the indifferent player.

Then, again, the forgers of iron heads are ingenious persons, and make matters easier for us than they once were. Not so very long ago the niblick had a face not much larger than a half-crown, and a man had to be very brave and quite unappalled by the possibilities of socketing to play a pitch with this instrument. Failing that, he had to lay the face of his lofting iron well back—he had not even a mashie—and cut the ball up into the air as best he could. Now the kind clubmaker gives him a vast saucer-faced niblick with which to perform this operation with the minimum of effort. If this stroke were more effective as well as easier to play than the cut stroke with the mashie, it would be impossible to find fault with it. But it is not so effective, since when the ground grows as hard as adamant the ball that is merely tossed high into the air will not bite, but bounces away into distant bunkers. The only ball that makes any serious effort to stop on the green is the one that is cut. At

Prestwick during the summer of 1911, when the ground was as hard and as keen as glass, Mr. Hilton could pitch the ball on to the 6th green and make it stay there; his younger competitors could not. Moreover, there are none among the younger generation of amateurs to be compared as artists in approaching with those pupils in an older and sterner school, Mr. Ball, Mr. Hutchinson, Mr. Laidlay, and Mr. Hilton. The niblick is a convenient short cut, but one that does not lead to the top of the tree.

The moral of this tirade is just this: that an occasional drive-and-pitch hole is not only a very amusing one, but a very good one educationally, if only the pitch be made difficult enough. The old drive-and-pitch hole was rightly despised and rejected, but the reason of its unpopularity was often misstated. The explanation given was that it was "a bad length." The real fact was that the pitch was not difficult enough; the bunker was put at just such a distance from the flag as to be as nearly futile as any bunker can be. This fact has been appreciated by the ingenious architect of today, and he occasionally gives us pitches to play which are almost ludicrous in their shortness, and yet infinitely alarming. Mr. Colt has made one—I think it is the 11th—at Swinley Forest, and there are two of Mr. Herbert Fowler's designing at Delamere Forest that come to mind. The point of these holes is that the bunker is very close to the hole and there is bad trouble beyond the green: the player has got to make the ball pitch just over that bunker and stop on the green, and—this is important—he has no way of sneaking round with his wooden putter. It is the kind of pitch he could play very comfortably over a lawn-tennis net with nobody looking at him, but in a real game he does not like it at all; wherefore it is extremely good for him and makes him, through wider experience, a better golfer.

There is one course that hardly any amateurs have played upon, and it is a piece of early education of which they feel the want all their lives. This course is the strip of rough, bare, stony ground, with hardly a blade of grass upon it, that is to be found in the neighbourhood of the caddies' quarters at nearly every golf club. There we see two or three small boys playing old, black and battered balls into holes of their own construction, and, unless, indeed, we suspect them of covertly using our own clubs, we pass them carelessly by. We do not realise that it is that ridiculous little course and others like it that breed the masters of the mashie. Yet so it is, for even the least alarming professionals have a control over the mashie that most amateurs must envy. Especially is the professional skilful at chipping a clean-lying ball out of a bunker, a shot at which the amateur too often boggles. The reason is to be found generally in constant chipping practice, but more particularly in the rough and bare and stony nature of the practising ground. On such ground the ball must be hit cleanly, and also crisply, or it will be utterly "fluffed;" wherefore the small caddie, impelled by necessity, learns to hit quite cleanly, and thus acquires a confidence and firmness of touch which he never loses.

For the young amateur the best substitute is a garden course where, if it be allowed, he can play many break-neck pitches over the paternal flower beds, or, as in one case that I know of, over the greenhouse. But in a garden the grass is soft and flattering, and the ball sits up as if desiring to be hit. It is much better than nothing, but the more sterile country by the caddies' shed is the best school.

One feature of a course which is likely to have a marked effect upon the game of its golfing sons is the size of the putting greens. The man who has been brought up on a course of big greens revels in his wooden putter, and the farther from the hole he can take it the better he will be pleased. He whose native greens are small will have a certain skill in chipping the ball from the edge of the green with the mashie, but will always feel rather lost and hopeless if compelled to take his putter at a range of fifty yards from the hole. If I may quote myself as an example, I was brought up for the most part on courses having very small greens. As a result, I would far rather play a little chip-and-run or "scuffle"—call it what you will—with a mashie than one of those dreary long putts. I am, I think, more likely to lay the ball dead with the mashie; besides, the long putt bores me, presumably because I cannot play it.

On all sorts of courses, and in all sorts of weather, the man who prefers the little chip may have something of an advantage. He is not quite so entirely at the mercy of mud and worm-casts as is the skilful wielder of the wooden putter. On the other hand, given a good course and dry ground, the man to back is he who positively enjoys playing with his putter when the hole is so far off as to be almost out of sight.

As far as putting is concerned, there can be, I imagine, little doubt that it is better to be brought up on good greens than bad ones. It is true that when, after putting on some muddy and uneven meadow, we are suddenly transported to a sandy paradise we often putt wonderfully. But that delight in our changed surroundings, which for the moment has so admirable a result, cannot be advanced as a serious argument. The young batsman would not best learn to play a fast bowler by facing him on a particularly bumpy wicket. He would have all the courage knocked out of him at the beginning of his career, and a bad putting green has something of the same effect.

It is not so much that a bad putting green frightens the player as that it compels him to overcome its badness by some unorthodox devices. He has taken to putting with an iron or a mashie in order to pitch the ball over worm-casts, or perhaps in the vain attempt to stop it overrunning the hole upon some wind-swept downland green sloping steeply as the roof of a house. This device is moderately successful, and on those native greens of his he becomes a sufficiently effective putter; but his chances of being a good putter with an orthodox club upon orthodox greens are not at all improved, because he has been acquiring a cramped and vicious way of using his club. May I be egotistical and use my own case again to point the moral? In early youth, on such abominably muddy greens as those on the Athens Course at Eton and Coldham Common at Cambridge, I acquired the habit of putting with a heavily lofted iron. I can still putt with a lofting iron—rather well for a lofting iron—but not so well as other people can with putters, and I am a perfect martyr to the vices of the lofting-iron style, having my hands much too far in front of the ball and my nose much too near the ground. If providence had planted me near a good course, and a stern parent had insisted on my putting with a proper weapon, how different things might have been! How many putts I might have holed that I have ignominiously missed!

Nevertheless it is good to have an excuse, and in some ways I find it a consoling doctrine that the sins of the courses shall be visited on their children.

Chapter VII

Caddies

By Sir George Riddell

For some years past the caddie has been the object of much public notice. In an age when romance and humour are scarce he has succeeded in attaining a prominent and not undistinguished position. The newspapers and comic journals teem with accounts of his sayings and doings. He is invariably depicted as having the best of the joke or discussion, and the public derive a malicious pleasure from the belief that the poorer classes still include one class at least which is able to keep the millionaire in his place by the powers of humour and sarcasm. In print the caddie is famed for his independence and contempt for rules, except the rules of golf, which he is supposed to hold in great respect, and of which he is believed to be the high priest or oracle. Whether the literary and artistic reputation of the caddie is justified is another matter. Printing ink and the artist's pencil cast an interesting glamour over a good many things; but however that may be, the caddie having grown to be a personage amongst the rich and well-to-do, his welfare has very naturally become the object of a good deal of attention. The golfing conscience has been aroused. National and local "movements" have been established, and various schemes for the amelioration and improvement of the caddie have been evolved. The boy-caddie is most in favour with golf clubs. He is more easily controlled and disciplined than the man. In many cases he has sharper sight and takes a keener interest in the game. As a consequence, there is a tendency on the part of golf clubs to employ boy labour; but there is an uneasy feeling that caddying is not a very desirable occupation for a boy. There is good reason for thinking that it gives him a wrong point of view, disturbs his mind, and unfits him for other occupations. It is a blind-alley employment, and frequently leads to betting and other evil courses. Personally, I have no objection to betting. Every man must be a law unto himself in such matters. Most people will agree that it is undesirable that a youth, whose future should be a trade or business of some sort, should start life under conditions which are likely to lead him to engage in betting at an early age. It may be said that the same argument applies to boys who are brought up in a racing stable, but the distinction is that racing is a business with many opportunities for an industrious and able lad, whereas caddying is a calling which offers few opportunities for advancement. My opinion is that, with the exception which I will mention hereafter, it is most undesirable that boy-caddies should be employed. As a general rule, there are plenty of men available, and golf clubs owe a duty to the community, first to abstain from employing boys and youths, and, secondly, to employ men, who otherwise would be without employment—in which connection I may say that many old soldiers and sailors are available, and most excellent caddies they make.

However, many golf clubs prefer to employ boy labour, and, the golfing conscience having been aroused, various expedients have been devised for the education and advancement of the caddie. In some cases technical education in carpentry and other trades is being provided. Personally, I have very little faith in these expedients. A boy who can earn 12*s.* or 14*s.* per week by following an amusing and exciting occupation is not likely to take kindly to the drudgery of a trade. Technical knowledge is not the only requisite for success, which depends on character, inclination, and point of view. I hold strongly that the employment of boys as caddies tends to produce wasters, and that a person should not be so employed until he has tried his hand at other occupations. There is, however, one important exception which I must mention. A system has been inaugurated at Woking by my friend Mr. Stuart Paton and his able assistant, Mr. Martin, which has been very successful, and which is highly to be commended. At Woking the boys are taught greenkeeping and gardening, which are their primary occupations, while their secondary employment is caddying. Instead of loafing in a caddies' shed they are at work upon the greens. Their greenkeeping and gardening education is a part of their daily lives. It is not reserved for the evenings, as in the case of the technical instruction. I commend the Woking plan to other golf clubs. It involves a little trouble, but the results are most beneficial. In reference to the employment of men as caddies, I need hardly say that a good caddie-master, whether he be the club professional or a person specially engaged for the purpose, is most essential. Everyone who makes use of casual labour knows the attendant difficulties, the chief of which arises from the fact that the labour is casual. There is no strong nexus between the employer and employed. The great object, therefore, should be to establish a regular list of caddies who have something to lose if they misbehave. Different plans obtain in different clubs, and it is obvious that the system adopted must be made to fit local requirements. At Walton Heath there is a list of forty caddies who are entitled to precedence in employment, and to whom the club guarantee a fixed sum per week. Preference is given to old soldiers and sailors, and to Territorials. It is the object of every caddie who is not on the list to secure the first vacancy. This leads to good discipline. Very often the club employ 130 caddies, and when I mention that the bulk of these walk ten or fourteen miles a day to and from their homes, in addition to caddying two rounds, it will be readily seen that the club are employing a deserving class. The club keep a labour register, in which every caddie is entitled to enter his history and requirements and capabilities. The members are invited to avail themselves of the register, and employment is being found through its agency for a considerable number of men. The club work in conjunction with the Labour Exchange, to whom they send each month a copy of their register, and the Labour Exchange in their turn send the club particulars of any likely caddies whom they may happen to have on their books, although I may say that usually the club have more than they can deal with. My observations have been directed to the courses in the vicinity of large towns. I quite recognise that different considerations apply to seaside or country courses where the boy or youth caddies amongst his friends and neighbours. The Insurance Act is likely to have an important bearing on the caddie question. It presents all sorts of difficult problems. The attention of golf club secretaries and committees should be especially directed to the schedule of contributions and to the

Chapter VIII

Essay on Some Questions in Greenkeeping

By W. Kirkpatrick, Rye G.C.
First prize, Sutton's Annual Competition for Greenskeepers

Most greenkeepers will recognise the fact that there is some diversity of opinion on several of the subjects of this essay—varying views having been frequently expressed by our best experts at the work, who are well qualified to give an opinion on any subject of the greenkeeper's art.

It would be difficult to frame twelve questions the answers to which would open up a bigger field for argument—questions which have been debated for years without any universal opinion having been arrived at as to which are certainly right or which are radically wrong. Practical knowledge teaches us to appreciate the fact that what may be quite the right thing to do in one place may be just the reverse in another, where the variation in local and climatic conditions makes a different mode of working essential. The rainfall, character of the soil and subsoil, aspect of the greens, and many other items must be thoroughly weighed before any given line of action is followed or advised, and these things can only be known to the man on the spot.

It is difficult, if not impossible, for the man at a distance, and consequently with no local knowledge, to give an opinion of any real value, much less to lay down any hard and fast rule as to what is right and what is not.

I am setting down some of my ideas which I have learnt, and am still learning, from experience. That these ideas are to be carried out in all places, and under all conditions, I should be the last to assert. They have worked well with me, and my experience has been somewhat varied. Most greenkeepers know that it is not always that our ideas can be carried out, sometimes from financial reasons, sometimes from other causes, such as lack of labour and materials, and where this obtains we can only do the best we can with what we have; but in other cases, where we are lucky enough to be under a thoughtful and practical green committee and secretary, who provide the necessary materials and labour to carry out the work, unless we neglect our duty, the course of which we are in charge should be a credit to our committee, the members, and ourselves.

NO. 1 — SEED V. TURF

One reason which may be advanced in favour of seed in preference to turf is the great facility with which it may be obtained. Turf of good enough quality for the construction of a golf green is very difficult to find—that is, good turf composed of fine grasses and free from clover and weeds, and growing on suitable soil to match the locality in which it is to be laid down. The question of soil is an important one. It is useless to expect success with turf moved from a heavy, tenacious soil on to a light, sandy soil, or, as frequently happens on a seaside links, on to pure sand itself; and vice versa.

Even turf imported from a distance, and from a locality noted for the quality of its turf, rarely does well after a few years. Change of soil and growth under different climatic conditions generally kill out the finer and more desirable grasses and leave the surface weak and coarse.

The area from which turf can be cut (of a quality good enough for a golf green) is becoming more restricted every year. With the advent of so many new golf clubs, most of the turf good enough for greens has already been used for that purpose; and when one considers the little trouble there need be to produce a first-class green from seed, it seems to me to be scarcely worth running the great risk of failure from turf when success can be assured by sowing the green with seed. One of the reasons which the advocates of turf usually put forward is that the turfed green can be played on in less time than the sown one. There is certainly something in this, but not much. As far as my experience goes, there is little to choose between the two in this respect.

Given a green where the constructive work had been properly done and the seed sown at the right time, the sown green would present a true putting surface as quickly as a turfed one.

Most of the turf procurable is composed of fine and coarse grasses. The coarse varieties certainly grow more quickly, and cover the surface more rapidly, than the finer grasses of the sown green, though with a very inferior turf; and however carefully the turf is laid, some considerable time must elapse before it presents a true putting surface, which is, after all, the time to reckon by, and not the date when it is possible to putt (in any form) on it.

Another advantage of seed is its freedom from weed seeds. If reasonable care is used in preparing the seedbed, few really bad weeds will appear. The annual surface-rooting weeds are easily dealt with, and the others can be got rid of with the hand fork.

We now come to what is perhaps the most important point in favour of seed over turf—the cost.

Although little difference will be noticed in the cost of preparing the ground (for this operation is as essential in the one case as in the other), the difference afterwards is very marked. The price of seed of the best quality to sow, say, an acre would not be one-fourth the cost of turf for the same area, and labour to sow and rake in the seed not one-tenth of the cost of laying the turf. The cost of carting, beating, and rolling, after it is laid down, is an item to be debited to the account of the turf.

There is also another reason against a turfed green. Should prolonged dry weather prevail, however well it be laid, some of the turfs will part and make a lot of work to fill them up with fine soil to the level again. This will make watering both difficult and wasteful, as once a new-laid turf becomes dry it is next to impossible to wet it by artificial means; and, again, when the turfs part and the cracks have to be filled with soil the first heavy rain causes them to swell into their full size, and the extra soil creates an unequal surface.

These are some of the reasons why seed is preferable to turf for putting greens.

NO. 2 – SPRING AND AUTUMN SOWING

The advantages to be derived from autumn sowing are several. If a green is sown the first week in September—the weather being suitable—it will give the young seedlings ample time to establish and gain strength before the autumn frosts and short days come along.

The weather at this period of the year is generally particularly favourable to the quick growth of grass, the ground being warm and moist; so the young plant grows quick and strong, rooting deep as well as growing upward. Seedlings which have stood the winter get over the cold, drying winds of March in proportion to their root action being active and healthy or the reverse. Seed sown early in September should be in a condition to stand any ordinary winter, and start away strong and vigorous in the spring.

Following an autumn sowing, less water is required the succeeding summer. Grass with roots, say, 3 or 4 inches deep will stand a dry time far better than those with roots but half that depth, and so will not require the same amount of water as the spring-sown grass. Again, the seedbed is more likely to be in the best condition in September from the conserved heat of summer than in March after the frosts and snow of winter; also September is not such a busy month with the greenkeeper as is March, so that the work has not to be hurried along as it often is in the latter month. Another advantage attending autumn sowing is that the grass stands longer on the ground, and gets better hold before it needs cutting, and so many of the young plants which, in seedlings lightly rooted, are pulled up by the machine are saved. If the seedbed can be prepared during the preceding spring or summer, any weed seeds it may contain will germinate previous to the seed being sown, and may be destroyed by lightly hoeing the ground over once or twice; then the bed will be quite clean for the reception of the seed. The birds are not so troublesome in the autumn as in the spring, so there is a slight advantage this way.

The benefit to be derived from spring sowing in the South is not easy to recognise. Many of the advocates of spring sowing fix their data from too late autumn sowing—say, October or November. Spring sowing is to be preferred to too late autumn sowing. If the ground is not ready by the end of September, it is

18th bunker or Soup-Bowl, Rye

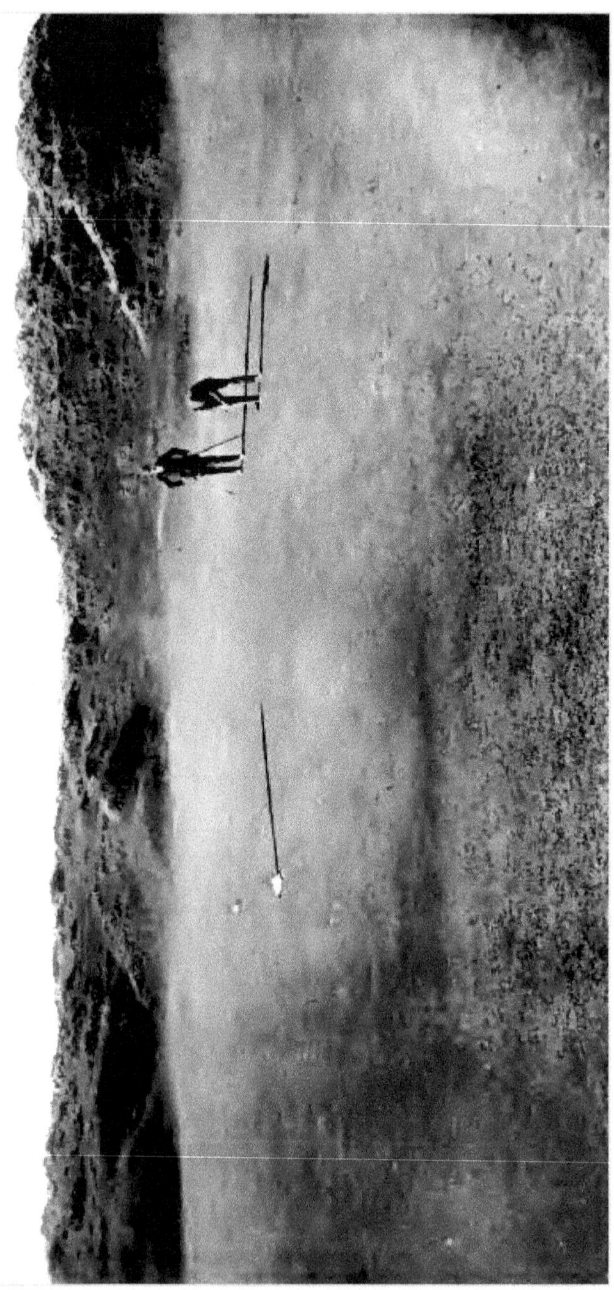

7th green, Rye

better to delay the sowing until March or the beginning of April.

Spring-sown grass is more at the mercy of the weather than the autumn-sown. More young grass is killed each year by sun and drying winds than by frost. There is little doubt that in a favourable season spring sowings are often successful, and with a smaller loss of the young plant from slugs and vermin. In the Northern counties and in Scotland, where the severity of the winters would sorely try the young plant, spring sowing is permissible, but in the South the only advantages I can see are those mentioned.

NO. 3 — MOWING

To produce a turf suitable for a putting green, and to keep it in true putting order afterwards, largely depend on the way it is mown. Nothing is more resented by the fine, tender grasses which compose a green than bad mowing. The object to be aimed at is to produce a perfect covering all over the green, and the way in which a green is mown has a great deal to do with whether that purpose is achieved or not.

When first starting cutting in the spring do not cut too low if the weather is cold and windy; a little grass protects the roots from the cold, drying winds of March. But great care must be taken in April, for if the weather turns warmer and the grass grows quicker, should it once be allowed to get long, a plentiful crop of bents will result, and the green be ruined for months. Use the box on the machine the first time over. Then if cold, dry winds prevail, let the grass fly. During such weather there will not be much to cut off. As the season advances and the grass grows more it will require mowing two or three times weekly, and must never under any circumstances be allowed to grow long.

Always change the direction of the machine each time it is used, running from different points instead of invariably one way.

Be sure your machine is in perfect order and properly set. If set too loose, it will tear out the grass; if too stiffly on the plate, it will run hard and cut in ribs.

A badly set machine does great damage to the turf, especially during hot weather; it bruises the grass instead of cutting it

The "Sutton" golf mower

Deal, approaching 3rd hole

clean, and the sun does the rest. Never allow the sole-plate to be low enough to injure the roots. It is better to cut three times a week moderately low than twice with the sole-plate scraping the sward.

One man can cut a green better than two; so have your machines of a size that one man can manage, and let each man keep his own.

A machine wears to the hand of the man who works it; it often happens one man can cut true with a machine that another could not use at all. A light sweep with a new broom before mowing a green is beneficial, and sets the grass up to the knives of the machine, and removes any refuse or stones. Never use a worn down or scrubby broom on a green. It will injure the young roots and uproot any young seedlings which may be coming up.

I am no advocate of a wheel machine on a green. On the fairways it is often useful, but the wheels mark a green and make it unsightly. There is no saving in labour, for to give a true putting surface to the green it will need the roller after the machine to take out the marks left by the wheels.

Always run right off the green to turn. The outside edges of many greens show up the bare places where the machine is continually turned. The grass usually surrounding a green is of stronger texture, and is not so easily injured in this way.

In conclusion, use a British-made machine of a good roller pattern in preference to the low-priced rubbish so often sold. It will come cheaper in the end, and turn out better work.

No. 4 — Box On or Off Machine

The time when the box should be employed or discarded must in a large measure depend on the condition of the green at the time. A man up to his work will see at a glance whether its use will be beneficial or not.

As a rule, the box should not be used in hot, dry weather. When there are any weeds or clovers in greens, or if they are troubled with the annual Poa, as unfortunately many are, it is best to use it; otherwise the seeds will be scattered all over them. It is not necessary for seeds to be ripe to possess the power of germination. This can easily be seen by observing the place where cuttings are thrown down from a green there will always be a good crop of seedling Poa in evidence.

Early in the season, when the weather is moist and the grass grows quickly, I prefer to use the box; but after the three-days-a-week mowing begins, and the weather is drier, it is best to let the cuttings fly.

The manurial value of decayed grass is of but little importance. It is in a protective sense that its chief value lies, the cuttings being a shield to the roots of the grass from the hot sun.

If the green is clean, it is a safe rule to use the box in wet weather or on a heavy green, and remove it on a light and dry one.

There is also a little difference in the time taken to mow a green with the box on and with it off.

It also seems easier to hold the machine to suit the undulations of a green without the box, so as not to cut too low on the hills and leave too much grass in the hollows.

In dry weather the protection given by the cuttings to the roots must be beneficial, and if the green is frequently mown, what little cuttings there are will not interfere with the play.

No hard and fast rule can be advanced either for or against the use of the box. Each green must be treated according to its condition at the time, the state of the weather, and the amount of grass to be cut; sometimes it is advisable to use the box, sometimes it is not.

No. 5 — Rolling

The proper rolling of a green is a very important point in greenkeeping. Before the evil results from the too frequent use of the heavy roller were recognised, there is little doubt that much harm was done by rolling too often and using too heavy a roller. A heavy green requires great care in rolling, and a roller of anything over 3 cwt. must only be used when the surface soil is dry. If used when the surface is wet, the soil will become bound down so hard that the rain will not get through, but run away to the lowest parts, flooding them and leaving the higher places dry. If practicable, the green should be given a good dressing of sea sand a few days before using the heavy roller, to be afterwards well rubbed in with the birch-broom. I am no advocate of the heavy roller on a green, but there are times when one good rolling with it will be found to be very beneficial, especially in early spring after a period of severe frost, which always tends to loosen the ground and make the surface uneven.

The heavy roller should not be used continuously; if it becomes necessary to use it, give one good rolling and then fall back on the light wood roller.

On an ordinary soil, or if on the light side, the danger of over-rolling is not so great; but even then caution must be used.

There are far more greens spoilt through over-rolling than there are from the want of it.

The roller is often used to collect the worm-casts, but on a well-kept course these pests should not be allowed to be in evidence, and its use in this respect is uncalled for.

Where the greens are mown with a wheel machine, a light wood roller following it gives a better finish to the work.

A good dressing of sand well rubbed into a green will true up the surface and make for good putting far better than any amount of rolling will beat it down, and will do away with the danger of binding the surface. To sum up the case, if it becomes necessary to use the heavy roller, give one good rolling in preference to following up with several light ones. Use the light wood roller each morning, unless the green is to be mown, and carefully sweep off any rubbish which may have been blown on during the night.

NO. 6 — WATERING DURING DRY WEATHER

In places where a supply of water can be obtained from the local waterworks and laid on to each green, this is the easiest method of solving the question. Unfortunately this is not always the case, and then some other means must be devised. Wells may be sunk at different points on the course and the water pumped direct on to the greens by hand or by an oil engine, or one or several tanks may be installed at higher parts of the course and pumped by a windmill or oil engine. These arrangements are, however, open to objection. Hand pumping is too slow, wind is not to be relied on, and engines run by oil or petrol are expensive to work, both in fuel and repairs. An oil engine of, say, 2½ horsepower costs about £75, and the running expenses about 7*s*. per day for oil and labour. Where the company's water is laid on, the only question to consider is the mode of applying it.

I have found nothing to beat the 1½-inch hose fixed to a hydrant at each green, with a fine rose on the end similar to that on a large watering can. By this means a man can easily carry enough hose to reach from one green to another, and the great advantage is that you can apply the water where it is wanted.

The idea of one man watering three greens at once is good enough in theory, but in practice it is a failure; for if he begins at No. 1, then walks to No. 2, then to No. 3, by the time he returns to No. 1 a lot of water will be wasted if it is running at any appreciable rate, and if flowing slowly enough to avoid such loss, the work will be greatly retarded. I much prefer to finish one green; then move to another.

Whatever method is adopted, it is best to water in the evening.

If sufficient labour is not available to water all the greens in the evening after play, it is best to let two men work all night and rest the following day.

In all cases a green should be thoroughly well watered, not merely damped on the top, as this encourages the roots of the grass to remain at the surface, which is just the reverse of what is wanted. It is far better to water only twice a week and give a good soaking than to water lightly every night.

If a green can be rested a few days during very hot weather, when it is badly dried up, it is a good plan to cover it with any flimsy material, such as light straw manure, rushes, or anything of a similar nature, and well water over the top to soak it whilst lying on the surface. It is surprising the quickness with which the grass recovers if it can be given a good soaking and friendly shade from the sun for a day or two.

I have tried many patent sprinklers, but my experience has not made me very partial to them. They can only be used when the water comes direct from the well. If the water is pumped into tanks, the scum which always grows on the inside of the tank during the summer chokes up the outlet.

The water from tanks exposed to the sun and air is much better for the grass than that drawn straight from the main, which is one reason in favour of tanks being used. It is also possible to put a bag of manure into the tank and give a little stimulant to the water, which is an advantage.

NO. 7 – ERADICATING WEEDS AND CLOVERS

Many of the surface-rooting weeds may be cleared out by the use of weed killer. The smaller patches of daisies are quite easily removed by this means, but where clumps of considerable size exist on an old-established green it is generally best to cut the infested area clean out and replace with good turf. Every course should have a grass nursery from which to cut for this purpose.

If large spots are dressed with the killer and the weeds all killed, the bare places will be too big to heal up readily, and so will have to be returfed. No benefit will, therefore, be derived from its use, it being as easy to cut out the live weeds as the dead patches. Where the patches are small, or in the case of isolated weeds, the weed killer is useful and saves time, as it can be relied on to kill the surface-rooting weeds. With respect to the deep-rooting weeds, such as dandelions, starweeds, and such, these can only be removed effectively by the use of the three-pronged hand fork.

Where undesirable grasses are troublesome, such as *Poa annua*, rye grass, and others, the work of getting rid of them is a slow job.

By always using the box on the machine when these grasses are in seed they may be prevented from spreading, and I have sometimes taken up a good number of the young tufts in early spring with the fork; but any means to eradicate them entirely must needs be slow, and the work tedious and expensive. All these grasses and the clovers can only be dealt with whilst they are in the seedling state, and before a new green is first played on is the time to get rid of them quickly and effectively.

If repeated dressings of nitrogenous manures are applied to clovers established on a green, and all the phosphates not absolutely necessary withheld, such treatment may in the course of time starve them out by repletion (if I may use the term) of nitrogen, the quantity of that element being more than they can assimilate, and the quantity of phosphates not sufficient for their requirements. I have found soot applied to clover does not much affect it either one way or the other; it has not nearly the same beneficial effect on clover that it has on grass.

If clover is very troublesome and no grass is growing amongst it, it is best to cut the patches out and replace with turf. Owing to the running nature of the roots, it is almost impossible to take up each individual plant with the fork.

It is useful to go over the greens in the summer months with the hand fork and remove all the runners from the outside of the patches. This will, at any rate, prevent them from spreading, and many of them can be reduced in size, whilst it also weakens the old roots.

Prevention is better than cure in the case of clovers on a green. Strong phosphatic manures should be avoided in making a new green, and as soon as the seedlings are large enough to handle is the time to have them up, and so save a vast amount of trouble and expense which will follow if they are allowed to establish themselves.

No. 8 — Manuring Greens

However carefully a compost may be prepared, much of its good effects will be lost if it is not applied at the right time, or if put on in a wrong manner. I am a believer in early spring dressing, and in the South of England from the middle of February to the middle of March is a good time. North of London it may be advisable to begin rather later. One advantage in early spring dressing is that if a green should not respond properly to the first dressing, there yet remains time to repeat it before the busy season begins, and, again, February is not a very heavy month, as mowing has not yet commenced; thus the work of dressing the greens can be amplified and more carefully done than would be possible later on in the season after the mowing is in hand.

Much of the dressing will be blown away and lost if the application is made during windy weather.

The properly prepared compost should lie in bulk under cover at least fourteen days before being put on. During this period some slight fermentation will take place, and it should therefore be turned once or twice; it is not advisable to let it heat too much, though a little will do no harm.

When the day comes along for it to be spread, cart it to the green and tip it up on an old railway sheet, which should be reserved for this purpose; this saves much waste of valuable material, which must happen if it is tipped out on the long grass.

One or two men now wheel it on the green in broad-wheeled barrows and spread it evenly and thinly with the shovel. By the time the last part is finished the first will be sufficiently dry to be rubbed in; this is done quickly and well by drawing an ordinary fibre doormat across it twice in opposite directions. If the compost has been properly prepared, there will be but little of it to be seen, and certainly not enough to put the green out of play. If it is the custom to use the light roller each morning, this must be suspended until a good rain comes and washes the dressing in; otherwise much of it will stick to the roller if wet with dew or rain, and so be carried away. The ideal day to dress a green is a still, dry one. The sooner the rain comes the better, once the dressing is spread.

Another handy way of manuring a green is by dissolving any soluble chemical manure in the water tank (where greens are watered in this way). It is during the time when watering is necessary that a little stimulant is very beneficial to the grass, when it is fighting for its life against long odds. Sulphate of ammonia is a useful manure for this purpose, as, being easily soluble, there are no bits to block up the rose or sprinkler.

It is not a good plan to use strong chemical manures unmixed with soil or sand. Many a good green has been spoilt for months through being burnt by using chemicals alone. It is also very difficult to sow in this way without putting too much in one place and not enough in another. Always mix chemical manures with at least three times their bulk of fine soil or sand. The other method may be quicker, but it is a careless way of doing the work, and the full value is not obtained from the materials used.

Another item to be observed is always to buy any chemical manure you may wish to use as finely ground as possible. Before it can be used in a compost the artificial must pass through a ¼-inch sieve. Some chemicals in a rough state will lose one-quarter their bulk in breaking down if proper means of grinding are lacking. Guano, as usually sold, contains one-fifth of its bulk which will not pass the ¼-inch sieve.

In making a new green the fact must not be lost sight of that it will be impossible to replenish the humus in the soil once the ground is covered with grass, and this fact suggests that a somewhat liberal supply of this great necessity to plant life must be dug in under the soil.

4th green, Swinley Forest

3rd hole, Sunningdale

A heavy dressing of good farmyard manure should be incorporated in the soil forming the top layer of a new green. It should not be more than 2 to 4 inches below the surface; this is deep enough, for if put too deep and dry weather follows, the young grasses, whose roots are still near the surface, will suffer from the want of that nutrition which, although it is there, is out of reach of the roots.

On a heavy soil, burnt material of any sort, such as garden refuse, old wood, etc., will be very beneficial, in a manurial as well as in a mechanical sense; in fact, any fertilising material should be used at this time which it would be impossible, or at least unadvisable, to employ once the green is finished and in play.

NO. 9 — COMPOSTS: PREPARATION AND COMPOSITION

The preparing and mixing of composts forms one of the most important items in greenkeeping; but although most of us fully appreciate the fact, one often sees work carried out in an off-hand sort of manner. The time when a good coat of road sweepings, with all the attendant rubbish and weed seeds contained therein, was considered a good enough dressing for a putting green has passed and gone. To meet the requirements of a modern green the dressing and preparing of composts must be carried out in a more scientific and methodical manner. As the labour in preparing and the cost of material fall heavily on the finances of any club where the greens are kept in good order, the greatest care must be taken to use only that compost or manure which may be expected best to repay the outlay. The natural soil of the district must be a prime factor in the choice of what will most benefit the green. To use a manure or compost, in any quantity, because it has been serviceable in some other place, perhaps under very different conditions, is, to say the least, an expensive and often a dangerous experiment. However, there are some well-known manures which generally produce the same result under any ordinary conditions, and there are also some well-tried rules which one may observe to advantage in preparing and mixing a compost.

One good way of preparing a compost is to build up the heap to the desired size in layers, one of well-rotted farmyard manure (if free from weed seeds) and one of light, sandy soil.

Should the soil be deficient in lime, this must be added some time previously, but never when mixing. If lime in sufficient quantity is wanting, the full effect of the other ingredients will in a measure be lost, as much of the nutrition it contains will be locked up and ineffectual. Always finish the heap with a layer of soil; this will prevent much of the ammonia from being discharged into the air and so lost. There should be a proper place provided for this heap, with a hard bottom to prevent the heavy rains from washing the goodness away. If run into a tank, it may be thrown over the heap from time to time, or used in a liquid state.

If there is danger of weed seeds in the manure, discard it and trust to chemicals alone; the same amount of nutrition can be got from the chemical manures, but no humus—a very necessary element in all vegetation.

One important thing is to be sure the soil is light enough. To dress a green with anything like a heavy soil is to ask for trouble.

If this heap is turned once or twice during the summer, it will be ready for use in twelve months. When required for mixing it should be cut down with the spade and chopped up fine. It will sometimes save time first to pass it through a screen or rough sieve before the last sifting. If the heap has been properly attended to, by the end of twelve months it will easily pass through the ¼-inch sieve if it be dry; if not, use the larger one first, in preference to using it on the green in any way rough. After the soil has gone through this process it is then ready for mixing; and next comes the question as to what chemical manure shall be used, for chemical manure of some kind, except in the opinion of a few cranks, is generally considered necessary to keep a green in first-class order all the year through.

There is no manure which will always produce the same effect and prove equally beneficial on all soils; there are many that can be relied on under any ordinary conditions, but the best cannot be expected to give similar results on stiff clay or pure sand as they would on good light loam.

It is at all times more satisfactory to obtain a grass manure from a first-class seed house; it is better mixed, and the proportion of the different chemicals composing it better balanced, than could be reasonably expected if prepared by any ordinary greenkeeper. The expert has the advantage of the amateur in this as in other difficult things, and whilst there are many greenkeepers well able to mix their own, it is generally most satisfactory to leave this to the expert. However, if it is desired to incorporate the chemicals at home, there are some rules that must be observed as to which will blend to advantage and which will not. In using more than one, it is not enough to know the action of each on the grass, but also to ascertain the chemical action of the one on the other.

Superphosphate must not be mixed with any nitrate, nor lime in any form with sulphate of ammonia or guano; basic slag must not be mixed with any sulphate or superphosphate, nor sulphate of iron with lime, nor lime with soot.

In preparing an autumn dressing on light soils, potash should form one of the ingredients. If the soil is very light, muriate of potash is best; if somewhat heavier, sulphate of potash answers well—20 lb. of either to the cartload of soil is sufficient. On some soils bone meal, at the rate of 1 cwt. to the load, is a good autumn dressing. Bones in any form are powerful phosphates, and encourage the clover, so must be employed with caution. Horn powder is much used on the Continent as an autumn dressing, and where it can be procured it is very useful on a light soil; I have noticed the effect of it for five years. Basic slag brings clover on most soils; but, apart from that, it is a serviceable phosphate on any but a calcareous soil. On light, sandy soils which are deficient in lime a good autumn dressing of gypsum or carbonate of lime is beneficial. As a general rule, any of the less soluble manures should be used in the autumn; the idea is to strengthen the grass after the trying summer weather and nourish it through the winter months. To do this it is necessary to use a manure slow in action, and not to force a strong growth of soft grass at this time of the year.

Whilst the compost or basis of the mixture for a spring dressing remains the same, the chemicals composing it may be different. The autumn dressing precedes a period of rest, the spring dressing one of activity and life, and requires a quicker-acting manure to make up to the plant the wasted energy which is attendant on quick root action. I have found the following mixture of superphosphate to be very useful on light, sandy soils: superphosphate, 50; sulphate of ammonia, 20; gypsum, 10; kainit, 15; sulphate of iron, 5 = 100. It is fairly quick in action and lasting in effect, and very safe if mixed with the prepared soil at the rate of 1 cwt. to the load. Unless the soil was of a sour nature, the result always proved beneficial. It is most important that this mixture be ground very fine and thoroughly combined, and it is well not to prepare more than is required for use at any one time.

Soot is a valuable dressing if mixed at the rate of 1½ cwt. to the load of soil; it gives a good colour to the green, and makes the grass spread out and cover the weak places.

I do not advise the use of nitrate of soda for a putting green. I have found it too forcing and apt to produce coarseness. On light, sandy ground a great proportion of it would be washed out of the reach of the roots during the heavy spring rains.

Guano is a splendid dressing on light soils. For spring use, 1 cwt. to the ton of soil will show where it has been put on to an inch; it is rapid in action and fairly lasting in effect. The Peruvian guano is the best; it may be necessary to put this through the fine sieve before mixing to remove any small stones and feathers which even the best samples sometimes contain. This must not be mixed with sulphate of ammonia, lime, or basic slag.

The ashes from any burnt vegetable substance are very useful as a spring dressing. I have known courses in France where nothing else but burnt refuse was used on the greens, and very well they looked. On many courses there is little to burn, but where any rubbish is to be had it is well worth the trouble of burning to procure the ashes.

It is often necessary to give a green a stimulant at the end of a long, dry summer, irrespective of the usual autumn application, or as an addition to it. In this case a very light dressing of a quick-acting manure is necessary. I have found Peruvian guano as good as anything. This need only be light, as it is merely to give the grass a start again, and must in no way take the place of the regular dressing.

No. 10 – Circumstances Controlling the Application of Certain Manures

One of the principal uses of malt dust is in a protective sense. A light dressing to a new-sown green will be beneficial to protect the roots of the young grass from the bad effects of drying winds and sun. Its effect on spring-sown grass is more noticeable than on that sown in the autumn. On a light soil, and in a dry, exposed situation, some little protection is very acceptable to the young plant to conserve moisture and to give a little shade to the roots. In the autumn it is not so necessary. I have found the drying winds and hot sun kill far more young grass than any amount of frost, and if put on late in the autumn, it is apt to stop evaporation and cause a sourness of the soil. Put on in spring, it is useful in protecting the roots, and also for its manurial value. Malt dust contains nitrogen and phosphates, and when thoroughly decomposed it adds humus to the soil. It should be applied soon after the grass is up; it will then be decomposed before it will be necessary to mow the green. It is quick in action and transitory in effect. In using malt dust it is best to give only a light dressing at a time, not more than at the rate of 6 cwt. to the acre, and repeat, if desired, in preference to one heavy dressing. Rape dust is often applied under similar circumstances, and is valuable in the same way as malt dust.

Sulphate of ammonia is usefully applied in conjunction with other chemicals in the form of compost. If used alone, a slight dressing might be tried on a green much run down by hard play at the end of the season—say, September—when it is desirable to produce a quick growth in a little time. These light dressings are of the greatest assistance given just when most wanted, and, being easily soluble and very quick in action, sulphate of ammonia lends itself well to such a purpose. When used alone it must in no way take the place of the regular autumn dressing, but only supplement it. A dressing of ammonia applied at this time would put new life in the green, but when used alone it must be followed by a more lasting mixture. The essential difference between a stimulant and a real manure must not be lost sight of. The contrast between the two is the same in the case of grass as that between a glass of spirits and a cup of good soup to a man—the one is a stimulant only, the other a stimulant and a food. I have found that if sulphate of ammonia is used on a green containing clover, it tends to make it look sickly, and I am not at all sure that, if persevered in, it would not kill it outright. Sulphate of ammonia is also used dissolved in water, and proves distinctly beneficial. Sulphate is of a damp nature, in opposition to guano, which is of a dry character, and so it follows that the sulphate makes a good dressing for spring use. It is extremely serviceable in conjunction with other manures, and is altogether one of the most valuable of the chemical dressings.

NO. 11 — USE OF CHARCOAL

The use of charcoal on a green is only necessary under certain conditions. When through the heavy character of the natural soil, abnormal rainfall, or other causes, the surface becomes wet and sticky, the use of charcoal is advisable. Another explanation of this undesirable condition in the case of many greens is the presence of earthworms in undue quantity. No treatment will produce a clean, firm surface until these pests are got rid of, after which a dressing of fine charcoal, mixed with half its bulk of sea sand, will be found very beneficial. It must be worked well in with a piece of wood nailed to a shaft, and moved up and down until the charcoal disappears from the surface. Another light sanding after the rubbing will be all the better. It will then require frequent rolling with a moderately heavy roller before the green will putt true. The work of rubbing in and rolling must be done thoroughly, or else the charcoal will wash out with every heavy rain, and leave the green unplayable.

There seems to be an idea prevalent that charcoal kills worms. As far as my experience goes, I have not found it so. The worms do not like it, especially if put on rather rough; but it does not kill them.

Any green inclined to sourness would be much improved by a dressing of charcoal, and it should be applied in the autumn in preference to spring.

The manurial value of charcoal is not great, and where it is used it should not be reckoned as a manure, and ought in no case to take the place of an autumnal dressing of compost. If a green goes a bad colour from any cause, a dressing of charcoal will soon improve matters and leave the grass healthy and vigorous.

One case where caution is necessary in the use of charcoal in any quantity is where there is any danger from moss. It has a tendency to produce this on some soils, and when left on the surface for any length of time forms an ideal spot for the spores to germinate, as I have often noticed in woods where fires have been burning. Any charred pieces of wood lying for a few weeks were covered with moss much thicker than the uncharred pieces.

Charcoal made from oak or beech wood is the best; that from fir and pine is of the least value. As a sweetener of the soil and an absorber of moisture, charcoal has no equal. Nevertheless, its use on the putting greens must be attended with care in its application, and when used in conjunction with sand the best results are generally seen.

For a green of, say, 20 yards by 20 yards, 2½ to 3 cwt. is sufficient for one dressing, and, as in the case of the composts, two light applications are preferable to one heavy one; let the first get well down before applying a second.

No. 12 – Resting Greens

Should a green be badly run down from dry weather or other causes, a rest would doubtless be beneficial to it. It is, however, only on courses where good spare greens are provided that it is possible to do this.

If a green is to receive any material benefit from a resting, it should be given during the growing period. To rest a green during the winter, when growth and root action are both suspended, is of little use; if the grass is not growing, it can scarcely benefit much.

If the greens are kept in good order and the regular dressing properly attended to, there should be little reason to rest them at all. The great disinclination of the average golfer to play on temporary greens often causes them to be used only during bad weather or after severe frost or snow. This is in a large measure due to the indifferent state of the usual temporary greens. If more attention were given to their upkeep, we should hear less complaints when the regular playing greens are closed. A rest is beneficial to a green that has passed through a lengthened period of dry weather or hard play. If it is possible to shut up a green (if only for a fortnight), thoroughly soak it and cover it over as previously recommended; it is surprising the difference it makes by preventing rapid evaporation and affording some little shade from the sun.

Unless the greens are run down, I see no reason to rest them. If during the periodical dressings the compost used is properly prepared and sifted, and, after spreading, well dredged in, there will be no necessity to close the greens on this account, as it will make but little difference to the play, and none at all after the first good shower of rain. Resting a green after the growing season is over is only useful to the extent of preventing the actual wear from the feet of the players, and cannot make much difference to its general condition. Should a green be in a poor, weak state in October or November, unless the proper steps are taken to enrich it and encourage the grass to fresh growth, it will be in the same condition in March, whether it has been rested or not. It happens sometimes that a green is in this condition in October or November, and all that is done to remedy the evil is to shut it up, say, in December for a month, and expect it to derive great benefit from the rest. A dressing given in October would have brought about an improvement, and in most cases made all the difference between a good green and a bad one. Rest alone, under these conditions, gives practically no result.

A rest at any time when the grass is growing will be attended with beneficial results; and spare greens should always be provided and kept in fair order wherever possible.

The soil composing the green, the amount of play, the weather, and the rainfall of the district must be governing agents to decide whether a green requires resting or not. Many greens require a rest after dry weather or hard play; others seem never to want a rest at all, especially if the soil is good and the watering arrangements efficient. But, for all this, it is a wise plan to have good temporary greens to fall back on, if through any cause it is desirable to rest the permanent ones.

Such are my answers to the questions asked. There is doubtless much more to be said on all these subjects, and I fear, in view of their importance, I have treated them too briefly.

Chapter IX

The Vegetation of Golf Links

By a Golfing Botanist

Golfer are a severely practical race of men, and the strenuous life which they lead on the links leaves but little time for observation in general. Such observations as they may have leisure to make are confined for the most part to those of a pessimistic or profane order with respect to the lie of the ball or the imagined inadequacy of the green committee. The eye of the golfer is keen to detect the glossy patch of clover which, if it occur at all on the green, is foreordained to find itself between his ball and the hole. Cuppy lies are the outward signs of the malevolent genius of the links which appears to be in league with that other implacable shadow of the name of Bogey and of the rank of Colonel. Yet among the great and ever-increasing army of golfers there are many who realise, albeit often in a dim and vague manner, that the conditions which determine the quality of a course depend upon definite laws, and that the changes which the vegetation of a links undergoes, although at first sight perverse and capricious, are, in fact, in accord with the principles which govern vegetable life in general. The many subtle and difficult problems which confront the greenkeeper and the green committee, though they may seem easy of solution to the uninformed amateur, present themselves to the man of scientific training as so many special problems in cultivation to be solved only by continuous observation and experimentation.

Every golfer with a habit of reflection has noted the general similarity which exists between one good seaside links and another. He has observed most certainly the many diverse troubles which befall him when, in an unguarded moment, he turns from the sound of the sea to spend a winter's day in seeking for his golf balls hidden in the mud of a heavy course inland. He remembers without enthusiasm the hopeless search among the daisies for a ball driven straight down the starry fairway on that same inland course in spring time. Although he be no botanist, the observant golfer with experience of many links recollects the very different floras through which he has walked in his various golfing pilgrimages. Despite his ignorance of their names, he remembers with pleasure the sight of the sea-pinks, sea-campions, violets, thyme or yellow bed-straw, which add so much charm to the game when played by the sea. It will occur to him that the gross dandelions which flourish, as though in Alpine meadows, on many a heavy inland course are not to be found on the springy turf of the courses which he favours; further, if the golfer's lines are laid on the inland sandy links where pine and heather abound, he is apt to discover with consternation that with the lapse of years a gradual change seems to come over the course of which it was once his boast that "it is never wet." It is true that nowadays, as heretofore, these links become bone-dry in summer, but this defect he may forgive; for although putting in such circumstances becomes a game of chance, his ambition of doing bogey fives in threes, vain and illusory during the winter, reaches, thanks to the run of the ball, proud fulfilment. But, as years go on, these same links are apt, in their latter degenerate days, to become almost a morass in winter, and a drilling ground for armies of aggressive worms. These phenomena, and many like them, are among the major mysteries which fill the observant golfer's mind with a sense of bewilderment. He may, of course, improvise explanations of the origin of these difficulties, though generally they are in terms of someone or other's inefficiency. He may turn the real or imaginary defects of the links to the purpose of explaining why what ought to be a scratch handicap remains year in, year out, hovering on the brink of double figures. On the other hand, it may soften his judgment and quicken his interest if he realise that in the changing circumstances of the links on which he plays he may see the embattled forces of Nature engaged in conflict one with another. The many and long campaigns which are waged by Nature's armies we cannot consider now; our only purpose is to show in broad and general outline what are the botanical conditions which determine the differences between good and bad golf links. To gain any philosophic grasp of this subject we must have some knowledge of the laws which govern plant growth, and of the causes which determine the distribution of different kinds of plants in different parts of the world. In order to provide an introduction to this knowledge, we may make one or two general propositions, not staying to demonstrate their truth, but assuming that they are well founded.

The first of these propositions may be stated thus: Floras—that is, the actual species of plants which grow in different countries of the world—are determined primarily by temperature. Some orders of plants love warmth and pursue it; they are the Macrotherms, and inhabit the tropical regions of the world. Other species of plants prefer a medium temperature; others grow best only when the temperature is low. We need not dwell on this aspect of our subject, since we purpose to confine our remarks to the golf finks of temperate countries, though to the Indian golfer the diverse temperature requirements of plants are facts of very real importance.

Our second proposition may be stated as follows: All plants absorb water and give off water vapour from their leaves. Some plants are amazingly extravagant in this respect, others are as amazingly economical. As an illustration of the extravagance, we may cite the case of broad-leaved trees such as the beech. Careful estimates have shown that a well-grown beech tree may give off as vapour in the course of a summer's day no less than a hundred gallons of water; hence it is easily estimated that an acre of beech forest transpires about two million pounds of water during the growing season, an amount which is a considerable fraction of the total annual rainfall over that area. Plants with this high rate of transpiration are called Hygrophytes, and those of the water-economising order Xerophytes. The latter class includes such trees as the pines, and shrubs and herbs, like the gorse, heather, and many grasses.

Our third proposition we express thus: Plants bear in their physiognomies evidence of their attitude towards the water problem. Thus mere inspection of the thin, delicate leaf of a beech or oak suffices for the botanist to realise that such broad-leaved trees belong to the class of reckless water consumers. Conversely, the fine needles of the pine, the leafless branches of the gorse, and the rolled leaves of heather and of certain grasses indicate that their several possessors belong to the class of water economisers or Xerophytes.

Our next proposition runs as follows, and is almost self-evident: The vegetation of a given country is determined primarily by rainfall. If the supply of water from rain or other sources be plentiful, the country is a land of forests and the prevailing form of vegetation is the tree. If the water supply be less plentiful, grassland takes the place of forest. If the water supply varies in different parts of the country, and if man does not intervene, those regions with the large supply will be under forest, those with the smaller supply will be grassland. In other parts of that country where the rainfall is yet more reduced, grassland gives place to desert. Unlike forest and grassland, the desert is an *open* formation; the plants which inhabit it lead a painful existence and are unable to populate it densely, and hence there is always room in the desert for any newcomer capable of existing there. Forest and grassland are *closed* formations; the ground is fully occupied, and intruders have difficulty in finding foothold. Between grassland and forest there is constant feud, and any small alteration of conditions may lead to the invasion and supplanting of one formation by the other.

Such changed conditions, for example, have resulted in the deforestation of great tracts of land in this country, in Southern Europe, in South Africa, America, and elsewhere. Changing conditions again may win the desert over to the grassland. For instance, although we have no extensive desert in this country, every seaside links provides an illustration of an open desert formation in course of transition to grassland. The fairway of the course has been won from the desert to the grassland. The dunes which form the ramparts of the links are moving in the same direction; the white dunes near the sea are still deserts. Here and there the most enterprising Xerophytes—as, for example, the Marram grass—are planting themselves upon the sand and doing the pioneer work of reclamation. Their spear-like stems, which pierce the dune in all directions, are binding the sand and providing the foundation out of which the grey dune with its scanty vegetation is constructed. Unless the forces of destruction, headed by the wind, undo the work done by plants, the grey dune is, as time goes on, invaded by other plants. Members of the clover tribe (*Leguminosae*) find a foothold there, and by their fertilising action enable others to succeed them.

Though we may spend no time in further consideration of the fascinating subject of Nature's way of making golf links, we may use the facts which we have just outlined to bring us to our last proposition. This is that over a region of fairly uniform rainfall the vegetation is also determined by the amount of water available to plants. In this case, however, that which determines the amount of water at the service of the plant is not only the amount of rainfall, but also the capacity of the soil to hold and retain water; for it is evident that, if a plant must obtain a certain amount of water in order to carry on its active growth, then not only must a sufficiency of rain fall upon the ground, but also a sufficiency of that rain-water must remain in the ground during the growing period of the plant. Hence it follows that in such a country as our own the final arbiter in the matter of vegetation is the soil. If the soil hold much water, and if much water be supplied to it, the forest comes into being; but if the soil hold little water, even though much fall upon it, it remains a desert, or at best an outlying fringe of the grassland.

It is not necessary for us to devote attention here to the science of the soil, since it is treated of elsewhere. We need only note that, although the rainfall of this country is, speaking generally, distributed fairly uniformly over it, yet, owing to the diverse nature of the soil, the plant formations which characterise our country vary greatly in its several parts. Those formations which depend on soil conditions are called Edaphic formations. Just as in the world at large there are forests, grasslands, and deserts determined by the amount of rainfall, so in the world in miniature—for example, in this country—there are forests, grasslands, and deserts determined by soil conditions. Our inquiry into the broad botanical features of golf links is thus narrowed down into the question "Which of the Edaphic formations of this country are suitable for links?" Any golfer who cares to consider the question in the light of our several propositions can answer it for himself. The broad-leaved forest formations must be excluded, for, though the golfer might be willing to sacrifice them, the presence of such trees indicates that the soil holds and supplies large quantities of water. That being so, the grasses which spring up in place of the felled trees are the sappy and rank grasses—in other words, those which consume the largest quantities of water. They show this habit of excessive water consumption by their rank and luxuriant aspect, and the golfer may know by their appearance, by that of the trees in the neighbourhood, and by the daisies and the buttercups and the worms that the grassland formation is there and is to be avoided. The fat cattle, the spreading oaks, the thistles and the buttercups, all proclaim that not there is the golfer's paradise. Hence we are driven to the apparent paradox that the good golf links is to be sought in the desert formation. Those who are not adepts at the game may perhaps declare that the desert is the proper place for all golfing Ishmaelites, and, though we dislike the epithet, the definition of locality is true.

We therefore continue our search in the desert for the site of the perfect links. As said already, the great formations merge one with the other; forest competes with grassland, grassland and desert combat with one another, and hence it is apparent that the golfer's paradise must lie on the thin fringe of land which marks the place of struggle between the desert and the grassland. In that narrow strip which the grassland is invading and reclaiming from the sea, the ideal conditions for the game are present. The soil is just rich enough and moist enough for the finer grasses to maintain themselves; nearer the desert of the sandy shore only the extremely Xerophytic grasses like the Marram grass may exist, while farther inland the rank grasses flourish to the joy of the farmer and the disgust of the golfer. Just, halfway between the two the more delicate surface-rooting, somewhat drought-resistant grasses find those conditions which enable them to exercise unchallenged sway over the ground. Nature has made the links and maintains them. The whole art of the greenkeeper of such courses is to allow Nature to take her course, and to intervene only when the fine grasses of the fairway show signs of being worsted in the struggle. Nearly all his ingenuity is directed to the management of the greens, but that is a technical subject into which we cannot enter here. On either side of the fairway the coarse bents which stand for punishment of pull and slice serve to signal the way in which the general and unceasing struggle between desert and grassland is progressing.

But, as all know, there are links other than seaside links which are good enough for championships, and therefore something must be said of those inland links which, like the seaside links, were earmarked by Nature aeons ago to serve the golfer's pleasure today. We say nothing of the moorland links, but will confine ourselves to that numerous class which occurs in the pine and heather region of the South of England and elsewhere. It would appear at first sight that a region of forests is no place for links; but the pine tree is not as the broad-leaved trees are. It belongs to the water-economising class. Pines of various species are used in many countries as pioneers of land reclamation from the sea. The health resort of Arcachon was reclaimed from desert dunes by the genius of Bremontier and the agency of pines. Hence the pine tree indicates an Edaphic formation suitable for the growth of partial Xerophytes, which are in turn the golfer's best friends; and thus it is that links laid out in the light soils in or about pine forests can hold their own, in their early years at all events, even with seaside links. But the problems which confront the greenkeeper of these forest links are more incessant, more subtle, and more difficult of solution than those with which the greenkeeper by the sea has to contend. The sandy soil of these inland courses is dry and peaty. It has no summer blankets of moisture like those which enswathe the seaside links. It suffers from drought in summer, and unless water be available the greens may become bare as boards. The peat in the soil is a source of trouble, for peat is tricky stuff. It holds water and thus makes drainage difficult. It dries out in summer, and if it decay too fast it provides rich food for ranker grasses. Hence, though when the links are opened the turf is ideally poor and springy, and the heather is at once a fearful hazard and a lovely sight, yet it happens not infrequently that such links tend more and more to lose their Xerophytic flora, and to approach by slow degrees the state of meadow land. Ours is not the task of prescribing measures to prevent this catastrophe; we can but condole with the greenkeeper and the green committee on the hard and unceasing toil which is theirs. Nevertheless it is encouraging to reflect that, as many links of this type testify, the encroachment of the grassland may be kept in check, and the original perfection and charm of the pine forest links may be maintained. This, however, can be done only by constant observation, cautious experi-

Swinley Forest, view from 9th green

3rd fairway, Stoke Poges

Chapter X

Finance

The object of this chapter is to give a few hints in a general way with regard to golf finance, as it is beyond the scope of this book to enter deeply into the subject. Clubs vary within such wide limits, and their aims and aspirations are so different, that it would need several chapters if the finance of all sorts and conditions of clubs were to be considered in detail. At one end of the scale we have an organisation for a membership of seven or eight hundred, with a palatial clubhouse possessing the conveniences and luxuries of a well-managed first-class hotel. At the other end we find a small club with possibly less than one hundred members, paying a subscription one-tenth the amount of that paid by the members of the more important club. Many will remember delightful days spent at a club of the lowly order, when sandwiches and a slice of cake formed the invariable lunch, with a flask of whisky brought in the coat pocket of the golfer, the professional's wife adding the sale of mineral waters to her domestic duties. Some may regret the passing—for it is now taking place—of those old clubs, when the clubhouse was called a pavilion, and the furniture consisted of a clean deal table down the centre of the room with chairs around of the well-known Windsor type. Rough lockers were placed against the sides of the walls, and possibly a small table in the window with homely writing materials, including a pen which had done duty since the club was started. The old red-coated *Golf* newspaper and its similarly clad readers were the only other occupants of the room. How some of those old veterans would start if they were introduced to an example of the modern Metropolitan clubhouse, with its elaborate luncheons, liveried servants, Turkey carpets, and soft armchairs! And the comparison which they would make would of a surety be invidious. The old type is but seldom met with now, and everything connected with the game tends to become more expensive and more luxurious. But so long as the course does not suffer, the popularity of the club, it is presumed, increases with the improvement of the cuisine.

The capital outlay in starting a golf club varies from £200 or £300 to £20,000 or even more, and the money is usually raised by the issue of bonds or debentures to those interested in the scheme. Sometimes there is also a donation list; the kindly bankers' help, too, is sought for a loan, and generally with success. It may be stated here that the bonds of golf clubs are by no means a worthless security. People originally thought that they were making a donation when subscribing to such an issue, but the annual return and the capital appreciation in value would compare most favourably with those of any class of securities during the last ten years or so. The instances of clubs failing financially are exceedingly few, while, on the other hand, we meet with many cases of great financial success, especially if the work has been done well in the first place and ample funds have been available for the purpose. This, no doubt, has been the secret of the success of the large Metropolitan clubs, many of which save considerable sums every year out of income.

Before examining financial details it will be well to consider the tenure of the club. But few have the advantage of freehold land; the vast majority are obliged to rely upon leasehold. However, the ideal position for a club is to own not only the freehold of the actual ground used for the clubhouse and the links, but also a considerable margin all round the latter. In Canada and America there have recently been instances of clubs buying the freehold of sufficient land to enable them to reap the benefit of the rise in value of the surrounding district due to the construction of a good golf course. And if clubs in this country were only to start a combined golf and building scheme, they would obtain a fairer share of the increased value of the land adjoining the links which has been entirely created by the facilities for golf. We constantly see building plots overlooking a golf course eagerly snapped up at prices previously never dreamt of. It is not overstating the case to say there is one instance of land, for which 5*s*. per acre could with difficulty

Le Touquet, 1st tee

The Hole Across, North Berwick

be obtained as rent prior to the advent of golf, fetching now £20 to £40 per acre ground rent. Moreover, the landlords take the whole of this benefit, although they never subscribed a penny piece towards the construction of the course. In this country an instance of a club deriving an adequate return from the appreciation in value of the surrounding district, entirely due to its establishment, is almost unknown. Therefore let those who are about to promote a golf club in a neighbourhood in touch with any large town consider most carefully this side of the question. If the freehold cannot be bought, a lease for a long term of years should be obtained. The usual term—21 years—is insufficient. There are no doubt difficulties when the land is subject to settlements. But even if the matter cannot be carried through in a manner to bind the parties legally, a written promise from the lessor, if he be a tenant for life, to extend the term of the lease at its expiration, the rent to be the same, is certainly better than nothing. A written promise is not likely to be broken, whereas verbal promises are frequently overlooked. A lease for a term of 42 years will give the club a chance of wiping out the original outlay on the course, and it is always feasible to obtain a 99 years' lease for the clubhouse land when a substantial building is to be erected. The future success of the club depends so vitally upon the tenure that no apology is needed for laying special stress upon this. Sufficient attention is hardly ever paid to the original negotiations—they are no doubt wearisome, and most golfers hate haggling. In the case of leasehold land the lessees have frequently to enter into covenants entailing personal liability, and, so that such liability may be distributed amongst the members, each one on election signs a guarantee to contribute a specified amount in the event of things going wrong.

If the capital is to be provided by an issue of bonds, we have to consider many points with regard to the conditions of the issue.

1. The property of the club will, no doubt, be vested in trustees, and, from the point of view of the club, it will be better that such property be not charged with either the payment of interest or the repayment of the capital. The deeds can then be deposited as security for a loan, which in the early existence of the club will surely prove useful. It is very usual now to charge the payment of the interest and the return of the capital upon

the surplus revenue which the committee consider available for the purpose.

2. The question of making the bonds attractive to the subscribers is not quite so important as it used to be, for reasons previously given. Free membership was frequently added to the payment of interest of 4 or 5 percent. But this is likely seriously to hamper the future of the club, especially if one of its objects is to provide a clear course for the members to play the game. More will have to be admitted to bring the subscription list up to the required amount. Additional inducements to take up the bonds can be provided in other ways. In a recent case a provision enabling a bondholder to introduce one guest free of charge in respect of each bond held by him has proved very successful. It was also coupled with certain rights regarding the introduction of lady visitors. In this instance the bondholders alone can introduce ladies to play on Saturdays and Sundays; this has already brought several substantial premiums into the coffers of the club. In fact, the want of facilities for ladies to play on these days can be taken advantage of in another way—by making it possible for them to become members if they first obtain a bond, and not otherwise.

3. We have seen during the last few years many instances of high premiums being paid for bonds, and if the club is a success there is every chance of this taking place. The conditions usually provide that the purchaser of a bond steps into the shoes of the transferrer, and comes up for election at once. If there is a long waiting list, many will be quite prepared to pay extra for immediate election, and this helps to force up the price. Under the conditions of the issue it would be possible to curtail the privileges of transfer to some extent. The subscribers might be placed under an obligation to offer their securities in the first instance to the club at an agreed figure, and the club would be able to participate in the increased value of its securities by reissuing the bonds at a good premium. For example, if the bonds are for £100, a condition could be inserted that the holders, before transferring them to a stranger, must first offer them to the club at, say, £120. If there were a long waiting list of candidates for election, the club would no doubt exercise this right of redemption, or rather purchase, and then reissue the bond at, say, £200. This is by no means an unheard of price for a bond for £100, as some have been known to change hands for £280.

It may be suggested here that the club should take powers for issuing about 50 percent more bonds than there is apparently need for at first sight. The expenses will of a surety be greater than is anticipated, and if the bonds go to a high premium the balance of the issue in hand can be placed with advantage, and the premiums used for redeeming the original issue, if not required for other purposes.

4. It is very important to provide that each transferee of a bond be subject to election, and not to allow the mere possession of a bond to qualify for membership.

5. The redemption of a bond will not usually determine the special privileges given to bondholders. After the club has paid off a bond the then holder will no doubt be able to exercise the privileges during his lifetime, but, of course, be incapable of transferring them to another. The rules of the club should contain special reference to the privileges of the bondholders, and provision should be made that such privileges cannot be interfered with without the sanction of a large majority of the owners. No doubt solicitors will be employed for settling the form of bond, and probably an agreement will be drawn up setting out all the conditions of the issue, and a form of the proposed bond be attached, which will be signed by the trustees and each subscriber. A copy of this agreement can be printed on the back of the bonds when they are ready to be issued.

The repayment of the bonds may be effected by means of a sinking fund policy taken out for a term of years equivalent to the term of the lease, if the land is not freehold.

So that members may obtain the benefit of limited liability, a company is very frequently registered. It acts as the proprietor of the club, and care should be taken that each member is also a shareholder in the company. If this is not so, it is possible that there may be trouble owing to the licensing laws. This is, of course, a matter for the solicitors to advise upon, and need not be discussed further here. Several of the large clubs which have been more recently started have not troubled about the formation of a company, which entails a considerable amount of extra work in connection with the necessary annual company returns and other matters.

The outlay must obviously depend upon the circumstances of each case. It is impossible even to arrive at any ratio of expense between the clubhouse and the course—the cost of constructing the latter will vary within such wide limits. If the promoters are the fortunate possessors of a site covered with good, sound turf, they may be able to spend considerably more on the clubhouse than on making the course. But as the success of every club depends infinitely more on the facilities provided for good golf than on those provided for a good luncheon, it is well to allow for ample funds for the former, even at the expense of the latter. Preliminary expenses, which include lawyers' fees, architects' fees for the buildings, and innumerable other items, invariably amount to more than is originally anticipated. The cost of making roads to the clubhouse and outbuildings is also in most cases considerable. Then the outbuildings, apart from the house, seem to increase in number as time goes on, and accommodation must be provided for the professional—very probably with a staff of clubmakers—for the caddies, for motors, for the greenmen, for the horses used on the course, and for the implements. Again, there are shelters on the course, and such luxuries as a messroom for the chauffeurs, and good roomy sheds for storing coal, wood, chemical manures, cases with empty bottles, and all the rest of the heterogeneous paraphernalia which seem to collect in spite of every effort to prevent them. A refreshment place where caddies, and possibly chauffeurs, can obtain at a low price food and drink of a non-alcoholic nature, and very likely a halfway house at the 10th tee to encourage weary members on their way with refreshments of a more invigorating description, may also have to be provided. It will not be beside the mark to say that if £5,000 is to be spent on the clubhouse and course, another £2,500 is almost sure to be needed for the innumerable other items. And if a club is likely to "tap" a large population, it will certainly be advisable to provide for ample expenditure if the prospects of the course warrant it: this must be the real guide. It may be judicious to spend, say, £5,000 or £10,000 on a scheme which is likely to provide the best golf in a thickly populated neighbourhood, whereas in the same district it might be madness to spend £500 on a course which would not compare favourably with those already in existence. To take another instance, that of heather courses, it would be only throwing money away to spend a few hundred pounds on such a scheme, whereas an expenditure of £10,000 might give an excellent return on the outlay. All these matters are purely a question of judgment, and

5th green, Stoke Poges

New 12th, Sunningdale

each individual case must be carefully gone into based on its merits.

The main points of the capital outlay have now been considered, and it will not be out of place, before discussing the income of a club, to deal very generally with the building and furniture of clubhouses.

Here again we see great variation between the requirements of different clubs. It is most important to "house" each club as far as possible exactly according to its present and future wants. In one, ample dining accommodation will be needed, and in another, with the same number of members, it would be wasted. Take, for example, a club in the Metropolitan district which members visit for the whole of a day, it being outside the "one-round" radius; and, on the other hand, take a seaside club with a similar number of members—say, five hundred—with hotels near at hand. In the first, very likely on a busy Saturday or Sunday there may be over a hundred wanting luncheon, in the other not ten. Again, let us consider the dressing and locker room accommodation needed in the latter case, and compare it with that required at a club near to some large manufacturing city in the Midlands. The members of the last named will be drawn from the professional and business men of the neighbourhood, and they will nearly all want to keep a change of clothes at the clubhouse for use after business hours. It would perhaps be thought not quite etiquette for the medical man to administer his drugs to his patients when clad in a Harris tweed suit: and an instance has been known of a bishop changing his pontifical gaiters whilst driving in his carriage to the nearest railway station on his way to play golf after a diocesan meeting.

The successful working of the house will depend greatly upon the planning of the service arrangements. The relative positions of the kitchen and the dining room, or of the cellar and the steward's service room, will do more for the comfort of members than the decoration of the club room. It will be well to keep the drink department a little in the background and dispense with a bar, which is so often monopolised by a few to the detriment of the many. One large room will probably be better than two or three small ones. Thus a well-ventilated club room of 60 feet by 30 feet, with possibly two good sized bay windows and two large fireplaces, walls with rough wood uprights with plaster panels between, without ceiling, but with the rough beams and joists and rafters showing overhead, would prove a fine feature in the plan. For a club of 300 members or so a room of this description would serve as a dining room and smoking room combined, and, owing to its size, there would be no nuisance from tobacco. How infinitely preferable it would be to the ordinary little dining room and the small, stuffy smoking room and card room so frequently provided! The plaster panels could be used for the names of the winners of the club's trophies, and for those of the captains and other exalted officials. They would probably prefer this to seeing hanging on the walls an unnatural looking enlarged photograph of their features as they were in their younger days. And if such a room were furnished with a little old furniture and the floor made of truly set bricks of a nice deep colour, with some rugs here and there, we might have a really charming club room built quite inexpensively in comparison with two or three rooms of the villa type. Or if something still cheaper is wanted, a clubhouse securely built of thick, rough wooden slabs, or of stout weather boarding with a lining of wood not of the ordinary matchboarding type, and a strong heather or straw or reed thatch, would cost but little more than the tin erection so frequently met with. Or, again, a wooden framework with plaster panels and an old tile roof will frequently fit in with the surroundings far better than the yellow rough-cast building often seen. There are many firms which now supply buildings at a low price without insisting upon employing corrugated iron. If artificial abominations in the shape of cheap adornment be given a wide berth, a substantial resting place for the members can be provided at moderate expense; and, further, much can be done in the way of a really wide verandah to serve as an outside dining room and tea room. Care will no doubt have to be exercised so that the club room obtains its light from other sources besides the windows opening in this direction. Dressing rooms of a suitable size, with lavatories and a drying room, also some provision for ladies, will be needed; and when comfortable but homely quarters for the steward and the staff have been provided, with adequate provision for cooking, etc., we shall have the complete equipment for the clubhouse proper.

The necessary buildings for the professional and the other accessories previously mentioned can be effectively and conveniently grouped with the main building: this will give a far better appearance than the detached sheds usually put up, which look more like an isolation hospital than anything else.

It is quite an interesting matter to compare the balance sheets and revenue accounts of various clubs—to see what proportion of the subscription list is spent on the course, how the catering works out, what has been taken for green fees, and all the other items which usually appear in such statements.

The first one examined is that of one of the best managed and most prosperous clubs in the country. The balance sheet shows liabilities of a few hundred pounds as against assets of several thousands. The revenue account certainly indicates a loss of a few hundreds; but in such a case it would be absurd to show a profit—the members would immediately ask the use of continuing to hoard up money. In this particular instance about 33 percent of the subscription list has been spent on the course. The catering account shows a good profit; but on searching through the revenue account we find that there is a heavy item in connection with running the clubhouse. Anyone who lunches at this club will realise that he is receiving more than is his due in return for the small payment demanded.

Next we may take the case of a large club in the North of England. Here we find that only 20 percent of the subscriptions has been spent on the greens. As a rule, the large clubs in the North spend less on the greens than they do in the South, and more on the clubhouse. The latter is used in many instances as a social club, where golfers dine and play cards and billiards, whereas in the South the social club is usually a separate institution—a club or a dormy house—and this allows for a bigger expenditure on the golf course. In the case now being considered, the clubhouse part is exceptionally well done, and after taking into account the receipts for refreshments of all sorts and for cards and billiards, the expense to the club amounts only to some £500; and this includes such items as fuel, light, water, repairs, renewals, and laundry, as well as the cost of the purchase of food and drink. The management is certainly to be congratulated on the result.

As exceptions always prove the rule, we will examine the balance sheet of another large club in the North where, with a subscription list of some £1,750, the amount spent on greenkeeping is over £800, or more than 45 percent.

Then we have a large Metropolitan club, where between £1,300 and £1,400 is spent on the course every year, the ratio of this expenditure to the subscription list being over 38 percent.

And now, for a change, we will take a small club in the Midlands. The subscriptions amount to a little over £400, and over £300 has been spent on the course, or more than 75 percent. The next one on our list is a seaside course on the South coast. Here the green fees paid by visitors exceed the subscriptions paid by members. The course has apparently cost about £600 to keep up, while prizes amounting to about £100 have been given.

We can now compare two clubs in the North of England. In the one case the subscription list amounts to between £800 and £900, and about half of this has been spent on the links. In the other case, the subscriptions come to some £600, and of this amount over £400 has been spent on the green account. In the accounts of another club, £350 has been spent out of a subscription list of £750.

It will be readily observed that the smaller the club the bigger the percentage spent on the green, but it is impossible to say what the cost will be of the upkeep of a links. There is only one safe rule, and it is to spend as much as the club can possibly afford—anything from £200 or less to £2,000. And if £400 only is available, it does not follow that double that amount could not be profitably employed on greenkeeping.

From the balance sheets now being considered, it is difficult to arrive at any general conclusions about the cost of running the house, as clubs differ greatly in the method in which the accounts are made up and presented to the members. Such items as laundry, fuel, light, renewals, and house wages are sometimes charged against the catering account, whereas in other cases only the purchases of food and drink are included, and comparisons are frequently made without sufficient knowledge.

As a general rule, if the house servants are fed at the expense of the actual food account, a very small credit balance would show good and careful management, and the profit derived from the sale of drink and cigars should go some way towards meeting the other expenses in connection with the house.

One thing is quite certain, that unless there be careful and adequate daily supervision, the cost of running the house will assume horrible proportions at the end of the year.

In conclusion, it will be possible to make up every month a statement of accounts for the consideration of the committee. The subscriptions can be divided by 12, and such items as rent, rates, taxes, insurance, interest on loans, implements for the green, repairs, renewals, etc., can be dealt with in a similar manner. The actual amount taken for food and drink and green fees can be inserted, as well as the cost of the first two and the amounts spent on house wages and green wages. Many other items will also appear, and the previous year's balance sheet will form the basis for the statement, which will prove invaluable, being a very fair guide as to the prosperity of the club.

Appendix A

Notes on Organic and Artificial Manures

The following notes on manures (organic and artificial), which have been of use in certain exceptional circumstances, may be of interest. It should, however, be remembered that all artificial fertilisers need applying with discretion and after due consideration of local conditions, and expert advice on the subject should be sought. A feature of artificial manure is that no danger of weed seeds accompanies its use, and, generally speaking, it is best applied in moist weather or watered in.

Sutton's Grass Manure is a valuable "complete" manure, which has been prepared in consultation with the highest scientific authorities of the day. When ground is being got ready for seeds it should be harrowed or raked in (at the rate of from four to five pounds per rod or pole of ground) a few days before sowing the seed. For an existing turf it may be used throughout the year either alone (at the rate of two to four pounds per rod or pole) or mixed with fine, dry earth in equal quantity. During the growing period the dressing need not be confined to one application, but may be used as occasion requires to stimulate growth through the spring and summer.

Dried Blood is a valuable nitrogenous artificial fertiliser for late winter or early spring use. Its action is gradual. It benefits sandy loam soils, and should be used at the rate of 3 cwt. per acre.

Rape Meal is highly esteemed, not only as a top dressing for young grass and newly-sown greens, but also on old turf in early spring, autumn, or winter. It is somewhat quick in action, and the effect of applying it is only temporary. It may be used on all soils at the rate of 8 cwt. per acre. It is nitrogenous in character.

Soot is a rapidly-acting nitrogenous manure, which encourages the growth of grasses. Its drawback is that it remains on the grass for a considerable period and stains golf balls. Forty bushels per acre is approximately the correct dressing.

Peat Moss Manure of high grade is useful for digging in on light sandy soils to assist in the formation of humus, and may be employed also as a winter top dressing, but should occasionally be raked about. Its action is lasting.

Bone Meal, Dissolved Bones, and Bones (½ in.) are generally looked upon as phosphatic rather than nitrogenous. The first and last named act slowly. Unfortunately there is great risk in their use, as they invariably encourage a growth of clover. Quantity varies from 2 to 6 cwt. per acre.

Muriate of Potash is, as its name indicates, a potassic fertiliser, and when applied, especially on light soils, where it is generally most needed, its action is lasting and somewhat slow; 1 cwt. per acre is the utmost that should be used.

Sulphate of Potash of high grade contains about 54 percent of potash, and is a useful manure for applying to land deficient in that constituent. It is, however, very apt to encourage a growth of clover, besides which it is generally too expensive to admit of universal use.

Kainit, although frequently employed alone, is, as a rule, best used in conjunction with phosphatic manures. It contains from 12 to 14 percent of potash, hence its great tendency to promote a leguminous growth; 2 cwt. per acre is a suitable dressing.

The following may be taken as the average commercial prices of artificial manures, but it must be remembered that they more or less vary from day to day. In all cases only the highest grades should be purchased. Unit prices are given on pages 174 and 175.

	£	s.	d.	
Basic slag	0	4	6	per cwt.
Bone meal	0	14	0	"
Bones (dissolved)	0	15	0	"
" (¼ and ½ in.)	0	12	0	"
Dried blood	1	0	0	"
Farmyard manure	0	6	0	per ton.
Fish guano	1	0	0	per cwt.
Kainit	0	5	0	"
Lime (ground)	0	1	0	"
" (quick)	0	0	6	"
Malt culms	0	12	6	per cwt.
Muriate of potash	0	17	6	"
Nitrate of soda	1	1	0	"
Peat moss manure	0	5	0	per ton.
Peruvian guano	1	1	0	per cwt.
Rape meal	0	16	6	"
Soot	0	2	6	"
Sulphate of ammonia	1	2	6	"
" iron	0	10	6	"
" potash	1	0	0	"
Superphosphate of lime	0	6	6	"
Sutton's Grass Manure	1	8	6	"

It is apparent that certain manures contain one ingredient only, but some of the artificials named lend themselves readily to mixing. Care should, however, be taken not to blend those which are likely to set up chemical reaction:

Kainit and basic slag
Bones " "
Nitrate of soda and basic slag
Superphosphate and sulphate of potash
" " " " ammonia
} will mix.

It is not advisable that any of the below-mentioned manures should be mixed:

Superphosphate and basic slag.
Guano and basic slag.
" " lime.
Nitrate of soda and superphosphate.
Sulphate of ammonia and basic slag.

It is invariably desirable to use the manures immediately after mixing. Another important point is that quickly soluble manures (like sulphate of ammonia, nitrate of soda, and guano) should be applied when the roots are active and able to make use of the fertilisers—viz., in spring. Basic slag, kainit, and bones, or any slow-acting manure, are better applied in autumn. "Little and somewhat often" is a good axiom to adopt; better results follow from frequent dressings than from one heavy dose, especially with the stronger artificials like sulphate of ammonia and nitrate of soda.

Approximate Weights of Some Artificials

1 bushel of Lime (average) weighs about 90 lb.
" " Kainit " " 82 "
" " Nitrate of soda " " 87 "
" " Sulphate of ammonia " 60 "
" " Guano " " 45 "
" " Superphosphate (mineral) " 66 "
" " Soot " " 28 "

Unit Prices of Manures

	Usual guarantee percent	Price per unit s.	d.
Ammonia in ammonic sulphate 95 percent	24 Am.	10	6
" Peruvian guano, sifted	5 "	14	0
" phosphatic guano	1 "	12	6
" fish guano	10 "	10	0
" bone meal	5 "	10	0
" dissolved bones	3 "	11	0
" compound manures	—	10	0
Nitrogen in sodic nitrate 95 percent	15 Nit.	11	8
" potassic nitrate 95 percent	17 "	14	6
" ammonic sulphate 95 percent	20 "	12	6
" Peruvian guano	4 "	16	0
" phosphatic guano	0.8 "	15	0
" fish guano	8 "	14	0
" bone meal	4 "	12	0
" dissolved bones	2.5 "	15	6
" compound manures	—	12	0

Unit Prices of Manures – *Continued*

	Usual guarantee percent	Price per unit	
		s.	*d.*
Soluble phosphate in dissolved bones	16 Phos.	2	6
" superphosphates	28 "	1	11
Undissolved phosphate in Peruvian guano	55 "	1	4
" phosphatic guano	67 "	1	3
" fish guano	26 "	1	0
" bone Meal	50 "	1	3
" dissolved Bones	20 "	1	8
" superphosphates	3 "	—	
" compound Manures	—	1	2
" ground Mineral Phosphates	60 "	0	10
" slag Phosphate	37 "	1	2
Potash in kainit 23 percent	12 Pot.	3	4
" chloride (muriate) 80 percent	50 "	3	6
" nitrate 95 percent	40 "	3	9
" sulphate 90 percent	50 "	3	9
" guano	—	3	6

The percentage of each ingredient in an analysis is to be multiplied by its price per unit (a unit being the 100th part of a ton, or 22.4 lb.); the sum total of all the ingredients gives the price of manure per ton.

Voelcker's Analysis of Farmyard Manure

	Fresh	Rotten
Water	66.17	75.42
*Soluble organic matter (ash)	2.48	3.71
" inorganic matter	1.54	1.47
**Insoluble organic matter	25.76	12.82
" inorganic matter (ash)	4.05	6.58
	100.00	100.00

One of the oldest methods of dealing with farmyard manure is to place it in heaps on the land. These heaps are made about 3 ft. high, but gradually sink to 2 ft. In some instances they are covered with soil, the object being to keep out rain and to prevent volatile products from passing into the atmosphere. The method is rather a bad one, and should be avoided wherever possible.

It is best to cart the dung direct from the yards to the land and spread it at once. On light, sandy soils it should be dug in as soon as possible.

Perhaps the best way of preparing farmyard manure for use is to make it under cover—that is, the manure should be removed periodically and stored in a separate shed, or in pits covered and made water-tight. By this method of shelter and protection the maximum amount of manurial value is obtained from such dung. The soluble nitrates are by this means prevented from being washed into the drains. The loss from volatilisation is reduced to a minimum. From chemical analysis and experience it has been shown that "box manure" is worth half as much again as farmyard manure made in the open, and about 40 percent less litter (straw) is required by using the covered method.

When forming a manure heap, certain details having a scientific basis should be attended to. The heap should have a clay bottom, or a thick layer of vegetable refuse or peat. The clay prevents drainage, and a layer of peat or vegetable refuse acts as an absorbent, if the soils in a neighbourhood are of a light nature. A good practice is to interstratify the heap with layers of peat, etc. (Griffiths.)

*Contains nitrogen = 0.149 = 0.181 of ammonia
**Contains nitrogen = 0.494 = 0.599 of ammonia

Composition of Animal Excreta

	Water	Organic Matter	Nitrogen	Ammonia
Farmyard manure with straw:				
Cow	77'5	20'3	0'34	0'41
Horse	71'3	25'4	0'58	0'70
Pig	72'4	25'0	0'45	0'54
Sheep	64'6	31'8	0'83	1'00
Mixed farmyard manure—fresh	75'0	21'2	0'39	0'47
Mixed farmyard manure—rotted	75'0	19'2	0'50	0'60

Composition of Animal Excreta – *Continued*

	Water	Organic Matter	Nitrogen	Ammonia
Peat moss manure	70'9	25'5	0'56	0'68
Liquid manure (drainings)	98'2	0'7	0'15	0'18
Human egesta–solid, fresh	77'2	19'8	1'00	1'21
Human egesta, liquid	96'3	2'4	0'60	0'73
Night soil–solid and liquid	93'5	5'1	0'70	0'85
Night soil–dried	11'5	37'4	1'80	2'18
Poultry manure–fresh:				
Duck	56'6	26'2	1'00	1'21
Goose	77'1	13'4	0'55	0'66
Hen	56'0	25'5	1'63	1'98
Pigeon	51'9	30'8	1'75	2'12
Town sewage	99'9	0'006	0'008	0'01
Town dried sludge	12'7	19'20	0'52	0'60
Urine:				
Cow	92'0	6'0	0'97	0'97
Horse	89'0	8'0	1'2	1'45
Pig	97'5	1'5	0'3	0'36
Sheep	86'5	9'9	1'4	1'70
Town sewage	99'9	0'006	0'008	0'01
Town dried sludge	12'7	19'20	0'52	0'60

Natural (Organic) Manures

In addition to farmyard manure other excreta are sometimes used, such as:

Horse Dung, which rapidly decomposes, and therefore its fermentation gives rise to considerable heat, being a "hot" manure.

Pig Dung slowly decomposes, and is a very rich manure. It is best mixed with other animal manures.

Sheep Dung requires a little longer time than horse dung for its decomposition. It is rich in solid matter.

Cow Dung slowly decomposes, and contains the smallest percentage of solid matter of the four animal manures. It is of far less value as a manurial agent than horse, pig, or sheep manures.

The following is given as the composition of the above-named manures:

	Horse	Pig	Sheep	Cow
Water	77.25	77.13	56.47	82.47
Solid matter	22.75	22.87	43.53	17.53
	100.00	100.00	100.00	100.00

Salt—The general properties of salt from an agricultural point of view are:

(a) In small quantities it promotes the decomposition of animal and vegetable matters contained in all cultivated soils.

(b) It acts as a direct plant food when used in small proportions.

(c) It has the power of destroying noxious insects, slugs, and weeds when applied to fallow land.

(d) It possesses stimulating powers on growing plants.

(e) It increases the power of certain soils of absorbing moisture from the atmosphere.

(f) It has the power of preserving the juices of plants and the soils on which they grow from the effects of sudden fluctuations in the temperature of the atmosphere.

Green Manuring—By ploughing in green crops (mustard, rape, turnip, buckwheat, rye, vetches, clover, and sometimes seaweed) the surface soil is enriched, first, by the constituents the before-mentioned crops have derived from the atmosphere, and, second, by the mineral and nitrogenous substances which the roots of the crops have brought up from the subsoil, and which are, by the act of digging or ploughing in, returned to the land. The advantages of green manures are:

(1) They bring up plant foods from the subsoil.

(2) They increase the nitrogenous constituents in the surface soil.

(3) As decomposition proceeds, carbonic acid is formed, which produces a disintegrating action upon the soil, thus converting some of the insoluble mineral constituents into soluble constituents.

(4) They warm the land, and add to its power of retaining moisture and ammonia.

(5) They promote the fertility of heavy clays by rendering them less sticky or adhesive, and make light, sandy soils more cohesive.

Compensation Values for Different Feeding Stuffs Consumed on the Farm*

Foods	Compensation Value per Ton of Food Consumed											
	Last Year			Second Year			Third Year			Fourth Year		
	£	*s.*	*d.*	£	*s.*	*d.*	£	*s.*	*d.*	£	*s.*	*d.*
Decorticated cotton cake	2	16	5	1	8	2	0	14	1	0	7	0
Undecorticated cake	1	13	9	0	16	10	0	8	5	0	4	2
Linseed cake	1	18	7	0	19	3	0	9	7	0	4	9
Linseed	1	10	6	0	15	3	0	7	7	0	3	5
Palm-nut cake	0	19	8	0	9	10	0	4	11	0	2	5
Cocoa-nut cake	1	11	6	0	15	9	0	7	11	0	3	11
Rape cake	2	1	1	1	0	6	0	10	3	0	5	1
Beans	1	11	8	0	15	10	0	7	11	0	3	11
Peas	1	7	4	0	13	8	0	6	10	0	3	5
Wheat	0	14	10	0	7	5	0	3	8	0	1	10
Barley	0	13	9	0	6	10	0	3	5	0	1	8
Oats	0	15	5	0	7	8	0	3	10	0	1	11
Maize	0	13	0	0	6	6	0	3	3	0	1	7
Rice meal	0	14	3	0	7	1	0	3	6	0	1	9
Locust beans	0	12	2	0	6	1	0	3	0	0	1	6
Malt	0	15	2	0	7	8	0	3	10	0	1	11
Malt culms	1	15	11	0	17	11	0	8	11	0	4	5
Bran	1	8	11	0	14	5	0	7	2	0	3	7
Brewers' grains (dried)	1	4	3	0	12	1	0	6	0	0	3	0
Brewers' grains (wet)	0	6	0	0	3	0	0	1	6	0	0	9
Clover hay	1	1	9	0	10	10	0	5	5	0	2	8
Meadow hay	0	16	4	0	8	2	0	4	1	0	2	0
Wheat straw	0	6	5	0	3	2	0	1	7	0	0	9
Barley straw	0	6	9	0	3	40	0	1	8	0	0	10
Oat straw	0	7	7	0	3	9	0	1	10	0	0	11
Mangels	0	3	1	0	1	6	0	0	9	0	0	4
Swedes	0	2	6	0	1	3	0	0	7	0	0	3
Turnips	0	2	4	0	1	2	0	0	7	0	0	3

*Reprinted from the article "The Valuation of Unexhausted Manures obtained by the Consumption of Foods by Stock," by J. A. Voelcker and A. D. Hall. Published in "The Journal of the Royal Agricultural Society of England," Vol. 63, 1902.

Appendix B

Tables and General Information

In writing a book there is often more or less surplus material which cannot be included under specific subjects. Some points of this kind are given in the following pages, and their inclusion may prove of service to those interested in matters pertaining to golf courses.

Drainage

In draining, the outfall is first to be fixed on; then a main drain should be run up every hollow—3 in. to 6 in. deeper than the others—and the small drains directly up and down the slope; 2½ in. in bore is the standard size now used.

The best theoretical shape for pipes is an oval or elliptical bore with one or two flat outside bottoms; but in practice cylindrical pipes are often employed, as they are more easily laid correctly.

They must be made of well-tempered, well-ground clay; well burnt; not too much sand in composition, and no lime; straight, smooth, and free from ragged ends; and should emit a clear ringing sound when struck.

The length of the small collecting drains should not exceed 300 yds. If the field to be drained should necessitate their being longer than this, then sub-mains must be put in across the slopes, so as to take away part of the drainage separately.

Rule for obtaining Size of Main Pipes—Multiply the square root of the number of small drains (of fair average length) by the diameter of small pipes; the product gives the diameter of mains sufficient to carry all the water when the feeders are full. In practice they are never full, and one-fourth or one-fifth this area (i.e., one-half this diameter) will be sufficient in ordinary draining.

If the distance apart of drains in feet be denoted by F, that in links by L, and length of drains in chains per acre by C, then

$$C = 660 \div F = 1{,}000 \div L$$

Number of 12-in. Pipes required per Acre at Different Distances Between the Drains

Distance	No.	Distance	No.
12 ft.	3,630	33 ft.	1,320
15 "	2,904	40 "	1,089
18 "	2,420	50 "	871
21 "	2,073	60 "	726
27 "	1,613		

Table of Size of Pipe Tile of Main Drain

Fall	Acres drained					
	3-in. Tile	4-in. Tile	6-in. Tile	8-in. Tile	10-in. Tile	12-in. Tile
1 foot in 20	18.6	26.8	74.4	150.0	270.0	426.0
1 " 30	15.1	21.8	60.4	128.0	220.8	346.0
1 " 40	12.9	18.6	51.6	108.8	189.6	298.4
1 " 50	11.9	17.0	47.7	98.0	170.4	269.0
1 " 60	10.9	15.6	43.4	90.0	156.0	246.0
1 " 70	10.0	14.5	39.9	83.0	144.4	228.1
1 " 80	9.3	13.4	37.2	77.0	135.0	213.0
1 " 90	8.1	12.6	35.0	72.5	127.0	200.5
1 " 100	7.3	11.9	33.1	69.2	120.6	190.5
1 " 150	6.7	9.5	26.6	56.0	97.3	154.4
1 " 200	5.7	8.2	22.8	48.0	83.9	132.5
1 " 250	5.1	7.5	20.4	42.4	74.4	117.0
1 " 300	4.6	6.9	18.4	38.2	65.5	107.0
1 " 400	4.1	5.9	16.5	32.6	60.3	90.7
1 " 500	3.7	5.2	14.8	30.1	54.0	81.6
1 " 600	3.3	4.7	13.3	28.0	48.6	74.0
1 " 800	2.9	4.1	11.4	24.0	41.9	65.0
1 " 1,000	2.6	3.7	10.2	21.2	37.2	56.0
1 " 1,500	2.1	3.0	8.5	16.8	30.8	47.0
1 " 2,000	1.9	2.8	7.4	15.0	25.0	40.8

Comparative Cost of Digging, Laying Pipes, and Filling Drains, at per chain of 22 yards, in terms of a day's work

Depth in feet	Digging drains	Laying pipes	Filling drains	Total cost
2½	.3	.04	.06	.4
3	.52	.04	.11	.67
4	.8	.04	.16	1.0
5	1.25	.04	.21	1.5
6	1.8	.06	.3	2.16
7	2.2	.06	.4	2.66

The Number and Weight of 12-in. Pipe Tiles of different diameters of bore that can be carried on an agricultural cart drawn by one horse

Bore of pipe diameter	Number of pipes	Thickness	Weight of 1,000
1 inch	900 to 1,200	¼ inch	11¼ cwt.
1½ inches	750 " 1,000	¼ "	14 "
2 "	500 " 750	¼ "	17 "
2½ "	400 " 620	½ "	25 "
3 "	300 " 500	½ "	34½ "
3½ "	275 " 450	½ "	40 "
4 "	250 " 400	½ "	45¾ "
5 "	200 " 350	¾ "	71½ "
6 "	150 " 180	¾ "	103 "
7 "	100 " 150	¾ "	120 "
8 "	70 " 100	¾ "	160 "
9 "	50 " 80	¾ "	180 "
10 "	40 " 70	1 "	228 "
11 "	30 " 50	1 "	251 "
12 "	25 " 40	1 "	274½ "

The first column of the numbers of pipes refers to those that may be carried in a cart with shelvings, and the other to those that may be carried in a long harvest cart.

Area of Bore of Pipes According to Diameter

Distance in inches	Area in sq. inches	Distance in inches	Area in sq. inches
1	.785	9	60.617
1½	1.767	10	78.540
2	3.141	11	95.033
2½	4.908	12	113.097
3	7.068	13	132.732
3½	9.621	14	153.938
4	12.566	15	176.715
5	19.635	16	201.062
6	28.274	17	226.980
7	38.484	18	254.469
8	50.265		

Mole-Plough Draining

The coulter of the plough has on the back of its point a "mole" or steel plug, which leaves an open channel behind it when drawn through the soil either by horse-windlass or steam. The channels thus made deliver into properly constructed mains laid with pipe tiles. The coulter can be set to any moderate depth, not over 3 ft.; while, of course, it is better adapted for pasture than for arable land. It can only be carried out on clays or stiff soils. The cost averages as follows per acre—drains 8 yds. apart:

	£	*s.*	*d.*
605 yds. At ¼*d.* per yard	0	12	6
Cutting main drains	0	4	6
Pipes	0	5	0
Labour, coals, etc.	0	3	0
	1	5	0

The following table applies only to drains in which the soil is easily cut by the ordinary draining spade. For drains requiring the use of picks, or in very hard soil, an allowance of from 30 percent to 50 percent additional must be made for the cutting and filling. The same conditions apply to cutting open ditches. A man at piece-work expects to earn at least 3*s.* per day and up to 4*s.*

Drainage Data

	Depth in ft.	Drainage apart in ft.	Rods per acre	Cost per rod
				d.
Very stiff clay	2.5	12	220	8½
Stiff clay	2.5	15	176	8
Friable clay	2.5	18	146	7½
Soft clay	2.75	21	125	7½
Loamy clay	3.0	21	125	8
Loam and gravel	3.25	27	97	8½
Light loam	3.5	33	80	9
Sandy loam	3.75	40	66	9
Sand and gravel	4.0	50	52	9½
Coarse gravel	4.5	60	44	10

Hill Draining

Open trenches 24 in. wide at top, 16 in. deep, and 6 in. wide at bottom; turf laid 10 in. from side, and clearings thrown beyond this. Trenches to be from 9 yds. apart on best land up to 35 yds. on poor or peaty surfaces. On "draw-bent" (*Eriophorum angustifolium)* or "moss-crop" (*Sphagnum acutifolium*) peat mosses, the drains must be 60 yds. apart, else these plants—valuable for spring feeding of sheep—will be destroyed. Cost up to 1*d.* per yd. to cut.

Results of draining are:
1. Soils are more easily and sooner worked.
2. Lime and manures act better.
3. Seed time and harvest are earlier.
4. Larger and better crops are obtained.
5. Good natural grasses spring up.
6. Green cropping can be introduced, and
7. Bare-fallowing very largely done away with.
8. The climate becomes warmer.
9. There are fewer noxious insects.
10. The health of the livestock is improved.

Cost of Cultivation

It should always be remembered that the preparation of land for a golf course is vastly different from ordinary field cultivation. The former may amount to £10 or £12 per acre, the latter to not more than £2 10*s*. The following approximate figures may prove interesting; but we would reiterate the fact that the cost of cultivation depends on the nature of the soil and the number of horses and men employed. The figures stated below are approximate only.

Ploughing costs about 13*s*. per acre, three-quarters to one acre being ploughed per day of eight hours.

Digging–To dig an acre of cultivated land takes a man a full fortnight, costing about 50*s*.

Trenching (bastard) will require nearly double the labour of surface digging; (full) costs generally two and a half times as much as surface digging.

Cultivation mixes and pulverises soil, does not bring up raw soil or bury fine top-mould; on light land three horses with nine-tine spring-tooth grubber can cultivate one acre per hour 3 in. to 5 in. deep. Cost, 4*s*. 6*d*. per acre.

Sowing–Ten acres of land drilled per day of eight hours, using two or three horses and two men: Cost, 2*s*. per acre. Broadcasted by hand, twelve acres per day of eight hours: Cost, 4*d*. per acre.

Harrowing–Ten acres per day of eight hours: Cost, 1*s*. 2*d*. per acre.

Rolling–Eight to ten acres per day of eight hours: Cost, 1*s*. 2*d*. per acre.

Water to Greens

Although the initial outlay is great, it is invariably of immense benefit to have water at hand when necessity arises. The supply can be secured by the usual method of service pipes or by windmill. The danger of pipes freezing in winter is minimised if the laying is performed in a workmanlike way, and they are emptied or drained on the approach of winter. The cost depends on the means adopted to obtain a supply of water and the nature of the soil.

GERMINATION OF SEEDS

Suitable temperature, moisture, and air are requisite for growth or germination. Seeds should be thinly covered with soil to protect them from the light. Provided the necessary heat, air, and moisture are present, they sprout, the radicle descending to form the root, and the plumule ascending to form the stem with its appendages. In sowing seed, Nature should be copied, and it should not be buried too deeply or access of air is prevented, which delays, either wholly or partially, the growth of the young plant. Seeds should be sown at even and moderate depths, never more than 2 in., but varying according to size of seed, and most varieties close to the surface. At a depth of 7 in. or more no seeds will germinate; but the vitality or ability to sprout is only suspended, and if brought nearer the surface they will probably grow. Grass seeds will germinate and become established when they are merely pressed upon the surface of the earth, provided they are not consumed by birds or scorched under a hot sun. The necessity of a fine soil and shallow sowing is obvious.

Various Grasses

	Depth of roots: average	Germination of seeds in open ground	Weight per bushel
	inches	days	lbs.
Agrostis vulgaris (Common Bent Grass)	3*	10	18
Alopecurus pratensis (Meadow Foxtail)	6	16	9-14
Ammophila arundinacea (Sea Reed or Mat Grass)	8*	21	15
Anthoxanthum odoratum (Sweet Vernal)	4	15	10
Avena flavescens (Yellow Oat Grass)	4*	15	6
Cynosurus cristatus (Crested Dog's-tail)	4	10	35
Elymus arenarius (Upright Sea Lyme Grass)	8*	21	9
Festuca duriuscula (Hard Fescue)	3	7-10	16-22
" ovina (Sheep's Fescue)	4	7-14	20
" " tenuifolia (Fine-leaved Sheep Fescue)	2	12	25
" rubra (Red Fescue)	4*	10	28

Various Grasses – *Continued*

	Depth of roots: average	Germination of seeds in open ground	Weight per bushel
	inches	days	lbs.
Lolium perenne Suttoni (Dwarf Perennial Rye Grass)	6	6	32-40
" pratensis (Smooth-stalked Meadow Grass)	5*	14	28-32
" trivialis (Rough-stalked Meadow Grass)	5*	10	24-36

N.B.—The above figures are approximate only. Roots of grasses vary according to soil; germination is influenced by period of year when sown and "energy" of the seed, and weight per bushel by the harvest.

Seeding

costs from £6 to £15 per acre, according to the amount of seed used; it may be sown, under certain conditions, through spring and autumn.

Turfing

costs about £100 per acre. 14,520 turfs, 3 ft. long by 1 ft. wide, are required for an acre of ground, and these will vary from 7*s.* 6*d.* per 100 upwards; if turfs 1 ft. sq. are used, then 43,560 are necessary to cover an acre of land. Turfs should be laid in autumn or early winter.

Clovers

Generally speaking, it is not desirable to sow clovers on golf courses and especially should they be avoided on putting greens, where they have a habit of spontaneously appearing and causing annoyance. The use of nitrogenous manures keeps clovers in check. If extreme circumstances arise where the presence of clover is desired on the fairway, there are three sorts which may be used—viz.:

White Dutch Glover (*Trifolium repens*), a perennial creeping variety, which is indigenous throughout Great Britain. If objected to, the best way of dealing with it is to rake up the creeping surface stems and scythe them off close at the crown of the plant, at the same time placing a pinch of sulphate of ammonia on the cut.

Yellow Suckling Clover (*Trifolium minus*), a very tiny-leaved annual species, and

Trefoil (*Medicago lupulina*), another annual sort, but apt to grow in ugly tufts unless well looked after. The two latter varieties do not amalgamate with grasses so uniformly as the first.

Yarrow (*Achillea millefolium*), which is neither a grass nor a clover, is useful on light sandy soils when kept under proper control and closely mown. Its strong, creeping roots make it an excellent binder.

SEA SAND

Being largely made up of decomposed shells, sea sand contains, in addition to its saline properties, a good proportion of lime. That is why it is so beneficial to turf, and assists in encouraging a fine growth. Ordinary sand does not have precisely the same effect, however sharp or fine it may be. As regards quantity, "a little and often" should be the rule; 1 cwt. to 2 cwt. per green (20 yds. by 25 yds.) once a month is far better than one heavy dressing.

FIRM GREENS

A cheap and effective substitute for charcoal (which costs about 70*s*. per ton) is coke breeze; the latter may cost anything up to 12*s*. per ton. Both charcoal and coke breeze are useful in promoting a firm surface; but they blacken golf balls more or less. Apply coke breeze I lb. per sq. yd.; charcoal about 1 lb.

TEST FOR LIME IN SOILS

Place two spoonfuls of soil in a glass, cover with water, pour on a teaspoonful of spirits of salt (hydrochloric acid). A gentle bubbling and a frothy head will appear if lime is present; if not, the land requires liming.

SOIL CLASSIFICATION

Soils containing one constituent are rare; nearly all soils consist of sand, clay, a small amount of limestone, and humus.

10 percent to 20 percent of clay constitutes a *sandy loam.*
20 " " 30 " " " " *loamy soil.*
30 " " 50 " " " " *clay loam.*
Above 50 " " " " *strong clay.*

A loam, therefore, is a soil consisting of a mixture of sand and clay where the ingredients are not much in excess one of the other. Chalk loam and gravel loam are soils where the chalk and gravel are the most noteworthy ingredients. A marl is a clayey soil with from 5 percent to 20 percent carbonate of lime; but should the limestone present exceed 20 percent, a calcareous soil results. A soil is most useful for purposes of cultivation when it is made up thus:

Sand 50 percent to 70 percent
Clay 20 " " 30 "
Limestone 5 " " 10 "
Humus 5 " " 10 "

There is sufficient sand to make it warm and pervious to air and moisture; clay to render it moist, tenacious, and capable of holding manures; limestone to give calcareous material and to decompose organic matter, and humus to yield plant food.

Analysis of Typical Fertile Soils

	Insoluble silicates	Alumina	Ferric oxide	Lime
Sandy soil	92.52	2.65	3.19	0.24
" loam (Dumbarton)	78.30	2.60	4.27	0.34
Loamy soil	81.26	3.58	3.41	1.28
Clayey loam (Essex)	81.26	5.46	4.60	1.23
" soil (Carse of Gowrie)	61.20	14.04	4.87	0.83
Marly soil	55.52	5.96	5.96	11.15
Calcareous soil (Salisbury)	28.77	3.31	3.31	30.55
Humous soil	72.80	6.30	6.30	1.01

BURNING SOIL

Stiff clay soils are sometimes "burnt"—i.e., the surface is taken off 2 in. or 3 in. by the paring plough or breast plough. Some straw and wood are taken to start with, and when the fire is well alight the soil is gradually added and kept smouldering. The object is to render the soil more workable, and to increase the fertility. The cost of burning clay is stated to be 6*d.* to 7*d.* per cubic yard of ashes.

Various Soils: Weight of Cubic Yard

	cwt.		cwt.
Dry peat	7½	Dry sand	22
Wet peat	15	Wet sand	28
Top soil	20	Sandy loam	24
Common earth	24	Marl	26
Clay	27	Common gravel	27
Gravelly clay	30	Sandstone	37
Shale	39	Limestone	40

CLIMATE

The average rainfall on the West Coast is 36 in., on the East Coast 26 in. The lowest rainfall is in Lincolnshire, 18 in.; the highest in Cumberland, 224½ in., but these figures vary from year to year. It is estimated that:

20 percent of rain falls in spring.
23 " " " summer.
31 " " " autumn.
26 " " " winter.

An inch of rainfall is equal to 101¼ tons per acre, or 3,630 cubic feet, equalling 22,622½ gallons. An inch of rain falling in 24 hours is about 2½ cubic feet per minute. When the atmosphere presses on the surface of the earth with the force of 15 lb. to the square inch, it balances a column of mercury nearly 30 in., or a column of water 34½ ft. in height.

Percolation of rain water varies according to soil, period of year, and other conditions. Taking the average rainfall as 28 in., it has been found that only 8 in. percolated through 60 in.

of soil, whilst 10 in. percolated through 40 in., pointing to the conclusion that capillary action had some influence.

The permeability or impermeability to moisture of various soils also affects the climate. Sandy soils retain little moisture, but clays hold from ten to twenty times as much, and thus render the air in contact with them cold and damp. Vegetation also affects climate, which is comparatively uniform and humid where the growth of trees and plants is luxuriant. The effect, however, varies with the nature of the vegetation; evergreens cause less dampness than deciduous trees, and grass meadows than ploughed lands.

The effect of winds on climate is very marked, for they bring with them the characteristic climatic features of the region where they originate. The mildness of the British Islands, for example, is mainly attributable to the prevailing southwest winds, which reach us after having traversed a wide expanse of ocean. Rainfall is an important factor, the precipitation purifying the air, and, for the time at least, decreasing the humidity. The frequency and seasonable distribution of the rainfall must also be considered. A moderate downfall spread over many days, as in Ireland, constitutes a wet climate; while a much greater rainfall confined to a few months of the year may be characteristic of what is essentially a dry climate, as in India and other tropical regions. The effect of snow is very marked. Being a bad conductor of heat, it protects the soil from excessive cold, but at the same time materially lowers the air temperature over it, so that the severest frosts usually occur when the country is covered with a deep load of snow.

Weeds and Coarse Grasses on Putting Greens

Weeds vary according to district, but there are a few which appear more or less common to most localities. Reproductions from photographs of six of the well-known and more troublesome varieties are given in the adjoining pages, and a few notes of other species of weeds and coarse grasses indigenous on many soils are appended, viz.:

Selfheal (*Prunella vulgaris*), which has a procumbent or creeping stem; stalked, ovate and nearly entire leaves, with purple flower. Prefers moist situations. Very difficult to eradicate. Should be boldly cut out.

Common Daisy (*Bellis perennis*) can be eliminated by the use of Sutton's Lawn Sand.

Plantain (*Plantago lanceolata and media*)—The former possesses lanceolate leaves, the latter oval stalkless leaves which spread closely on the ground. Both varieties are familiar, and can generally be eradicated by lawn sand when applied to the crown, provided the latter has been previously pierced with a skewer or sharp instrument. They can also be effectually destroyed by "Stellicide."

Plantain (Buckshorn) (*Plantago coronopus*) has spreading linear-lanceolate leaves, deeply divided and resembling a buck's horn. It used to be confined to places near the sea, but is rapidly spreading inland. Spudding out is, of course, a sure way of destroying it, or it may be killed by "Stellicide."

Chickweed (*Cerastium vulgatum*)—This is the most troublesome of three or four species, and should be treated with lawn sand.

Pearlwort (*Sagina procumbens*) is a minute grass-like annual weed which seeds itself so sedulously as to become almost perennial. Generally speaking, it is not objected to, and severe frost invariably kills it.

Bulbous Buttercup (*Ranunculus bulbosus*) can be destroyed by lawn sand if care is taken to pierce the corm. The only alternative is hand-weeding on a showery day, when the plants "lift" easily. It is a hairy erect perennial with a swollen bulb-like stem, and no runners such as *R. repens* has. The flowers vary from ½ to 1 inch in diameter, the sepals being reflexed so as to touch the stem. It favours light and calcareous soils.

Creeping Buttercup (*Ranunculus repens*) is extremely difficult to eliminate, as runners shoot out from among the radical leaves, and new plants are formed at every node. The flower stems are seldom a foot high, and the leaves are divided into three stalked segments, each one lobed and toothed, the central one projecting considerably beyond the others, so as to give the whole leaf an ovate form as distinct from the rounded one of the Common Buttercup. It is necessary to cut out this pest, as surface treatment invariably fails.

Bellis Perennis (Common Daisy)

Plantago Lanceolata (Plantain)

Plantago Coronopus
Buckshorn Plantain

Cerastium Vulgatum
Mouse-ear Chickweed

Prunella Vulgaris (Selfheal)

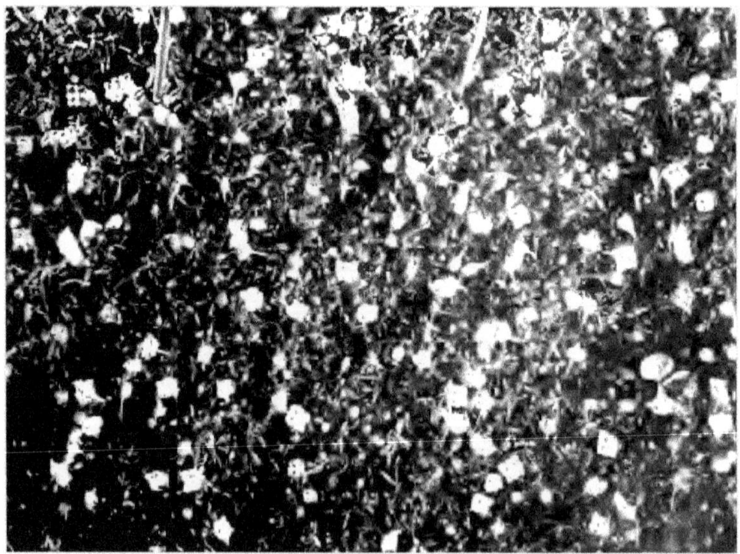

Sagina Procumbens (Pearlwort)

Common Buttercup, or Crowfoot (*Ranunculus acris*)—The well-known perennial variety common in almost every pasture. Varies in size, and is more or less covered with soft hairs, which are mostly spreading, but deflexed on the lower part of the stem. The leaves are nearly all stalked, and deeply divided into 3, 5, or 7 palmate segments. Flowers rather large, bright yellow, on long stalks. Sepals yellowish green, concave, but not reflexed on the peduncle. Stabbing the heart of the plant with a sharp instrument and applying lawn sand is efficacious, though sturdy specimens sometimes require a second treatment.

Dandelion (*Taraxacum officinale*) has a thick fleshy tap-root, and sometimes if the head is cut the roots bleed to death, but unless the root is cut well below the collar two or three heads appear. Lawn sand or "Stellicide" worked into the tap-root is sometimes successful, but spudding out is undoubtedly the best method.

Heath Galium or Heath Bedstraw (*Galium saxatile*) should be hand-weeded, it being a strong growing perennial which does not yield easily to any weed destroyers.

Shepherd's Purse (*Capsella bursa-pastoris*) is a common annual weed which appears in newly-sown greens, but invariably vanishes under constant mowing. Having a long tap-root, the plant is readily withdrawn by hand when the ground is moist.

Lesser Celandine or Figwort (*Ranunculus ficaria*) has fibrous roots as well as small tubers, which are capable of becoming perfect plants. Cutting out is the only remedy; care should be taken to remove each tuber.

Thyme-leaved Speedwell (*Veronica serpyllifolia*) should be cut out whenever a plant is found amongst the grass.

Parsley Piert (*Alchemilla arvensis*) is a small annual plant, its leaves fan-shape and clasping the stem like an inverted mantle, which accounts for its being sometimes called "Lady's Mantle." Should be raked out.

Common Fumitory (*Fumaria officinalis*) is sometimes met with amongst turf. It has a prostrate habit of growth with divided leaves. It sometimes becomes troublesome, but usually succumbs under persistent mowing.

Annual Knawel (*Scleranthus annuus*) occasionally appears, especially on light sandy soils, and if it once gets a hold quickly smothers the fine grass. The treatment consists in raking out or hand-weeding.

Field Madder (*Sherardia arvensis*) is often plentiful, particularly on light sandy, loamy, and chalky soils. It is a small prostrate annual, and quickly dies out if prevented from seeding by close mowing.

Groundsel (*Senecio vulgaris*) is familiar, and grows very rapidly. Its ragged, coarsely-toothed and cut leaves make it easily recognisable. Must be hoed or hand-weeded.

Yorkshire Fog Grass (*Holcus lanatus*) is a worthless variety readily detected by its broad, pale-green leaves. Cutting out is the only successful way of dealing with it.

Rough Cocksfoot (*Dactylis glomerata*) is another variety which has an unpleasant way of appearing in turf, and must be treated in the same drastic manner as the Yorkshire Fog.

Couch Grass (*Triticum repens*) possesses a strongly creeping root-stock, and is difficult to deal with. If the ground is properly prepared before sowing it is rare that this grass afterwards appears.

LAWN SAND

A preparation for the destruction of certain weeds, such as daisies, plantain, chickweed, etc., in turf. It is usually applied in dry weather at the rate of 4 oz. to the square yard.

MOSS DESTROYER,

scattered at the rate of ¾ oz. to the square yard, destroys the moss and encourages a thick growth of grass.

FAIRY RINGS,

which so greatly disfigure some putting greens, can be cured by using Fairy Ring Destroyer at the rate of 2 lb. per pole.

"Fairy ring" fungus, before treatment

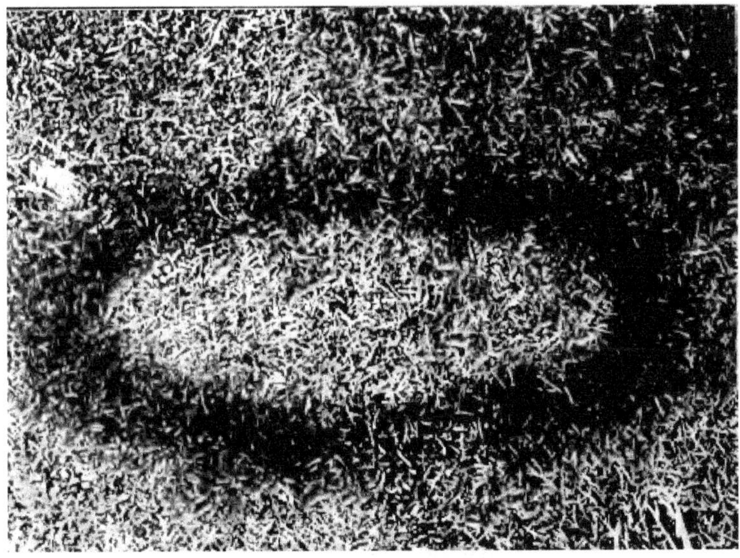

"Fairy ring" fungus, after treatment

Worm Destroyer

takes the form of a powder, and is scattered over the grass at the rate of from a half to one pound per square yard and well-watered in. It is invaluable for preventing worm-casts and nourishing the turf.

Insect Pests

In addition to the annoyance caused by worms, there are some forms of insects which do a great amount of damage to the grass family, and experience shows that when turf is once established the difficulty of dealing with such pests is increased. Probably the most common is that known as:

The Daddy-longlegs or Crane Fly (*Tipula oleracea*), which deposits its eggs in turf during early autumn. These hatch out very quickly, and become the familiar "leather jackets." These grubs at once attack the roots of the grass, the leaves of which rapidly assume a brown, withered, and very unsightly appearance. Vaporite is useful in destroying them, but unfortunately there is the risk of injuring the grass. Worm-destroyer is sometimes successful. Paris Green (a deadly poison) mixed with fresh lime and used diluted with water brings the grubs to the surface; but the risk of using this preparation is very great. Good rolling and the use of stimulating manures may be adopted without fear.

The Cockchafer Grub (*Melolontha vulgaris*) is another pest which attacks grass roots, and may be treated by forcing manures and plenty of rolling.

The Antler Moth (*Charceas graminis*) in the larva stage is also destructive.

Stem Eelworm (*Tylenchus devastatrix*), although not classed as an insect, causes a great deal of mischief. The eelworm attacks the stems of certain grasses and other plants. It is an obstinate pest to eradicate even when land is under cultivation, and the difficulty is increased when turf is invaded. A mixture of sulphate of potash (3 cwts.) and sulphate of ammonia (1 cwt.) per acre sometimes proves effectual. This should be applied in showery weather.

INSECTICIDES

A good many insecticides are now prepared and offered by several reliable firms. When employed as directed by the makers they generally prove very efficacious.

SHEEP GRAZING ON GOLF COURSES

Unless cake-fed, sheep return no benefit to the ground, but in sufficient number they help to keep down the expense of mowing and rolling. In this sense they prove an asset, especially to a struggling club. Against this must be set the damage done to the greens by "scalding" the turf, the breaking down of the face of the bunkers, and the objectionable fouling of the fairway, to which must be added the nuisance they invariably are to players. Altogether the advantages of sheep are far outweighed by the disadvantages.

FLORAL HAZARDS

In connection with Mr. Martin H. F. Sutton's article on grasses and grass seeds it may be stated that all the varieties he mentions can be grown from seed. Cocksfoot, Timothy, Fiorin, Slender False Brome Grass, Heath False Brome Grass, Reed Canary Grass, Meadow Barley Grass, and Awnless Brome Grass may be sown straight away where they are to grow, but for this purpose Upright Sea Lyme Grass, Sea Reed or Marram Grass, Gorse, and Broom should be raised from seed in a seedbed, and the seedlings transplanted when sufficiently strong. *Erica vulgaris* (Heather) is another suitable hazard for heath land and dry soils. Seed, however, does not germinate well, and wild plants must be obtained and transplanted.

CLUMPS OF TREES FOR OUTSKIRTS OF COURSES

An interesting question in connection with the making of golf courses is the subject of trees for the outlying area. Three varieties extremely useful for the purpose are as follows:

Birch (*Betula alba*) is especially suitable for Northern districts, and will thrive on damp soil. It matures in about seventy years, and grows fully 60 ft. high. The bark is used for tanning nets, and the timber is very firm and white.

Scotch Fir (*Pinus sylvestris*) grows well where the birch is the natural tree, and matures at eighty years. It prefers open, exposed situations, and does well on poor, dry soils.

Larch (*Larix Europaea*) does well in stony situations on hillsides, and likes plenty of room for developing. It prefers a mixed plantation.

Number of Trees to an Acre

2 ft.	apart	each	way	10,890	12 ft.	apart	each	way	302
3	"	"	"	4,840	15	"	"	"	200
4	"	"	"	2,722	18	"	"	"	135
5	"	"	"	1,742	20	"	"	"	110
6	"	"	"	1,210	22	"	"	"	90
8	"	"	"	680	25	"	"	"	70
10	"	"	"	435	30	"	"	"	50

Diseases of Trees

Fungoid Pests—Under this heading may be noted the pine blister (*Peridermium pini*), larch "canker" (*Peziza Wilkommii*), root rot (*Trametes radiciperda*), and tawny yellow toadstool (*Agaricus melleus*) as causing injury in some form or another. It may, however, be safely assumed that trees will invariably remain in a healthy state and not yield to the attacks of their enemies if varieties suitable to a given situation be planted, superfluous moisture removed by surface drains, thinning properly carried out, injuries dressed with an antiseptic, such as coal-tar, and dead branches and other rubbish removed and burnt.

Insect Pests—Amongst insect pests, mention may be made of the pine weevil (*Hylobius abietis*), pine beetle (*Hylurgus piniperda*), and larch aphis (*Chermes laricis*). The two former are destructive in both, beetle and larva stages, the last in the larva stage only. Pine weevils and beetles attack the young shoots, and may be destroyed by placing pieces of pine logs round the trunks to serve as "traps." Spraying with lime water is a good treatment for the larch aphis, which attacks the buds.

TIMBER MEASUREMENT

Standing Timber—The simplest and easiest way is to take the whole length of the tree to the height where it girths 26 in. round the bark. Then take the mean girth of the tree between this point and the base. If the measurement is taken outside the bark, 1 in. should be allowed for every foot of circumference. In practice it is usual to girth the standing tree at 6 ft. from the ground, which gives the medium girth of the lower 12 ft.; then compute by sight the upper part of the tree, which a little experience soon enables anyone to do sufficiently near for all practical purposes. Before commencing to measure, the forester provides himself with a foot-rule and slide, leather strap marked or graduated, a pole, a marking axe, and a red lead pencil or a small brush and paint. The strap may be any convenient length, from 15 ft. to 20 ft., ¾ in. broad, and of the strength of a small bridle-rein, with a piece of lead attached to one end of it. Previous to marking the strap with the necessary figures the leather should be alternately wetted and dried, otherwise it is apt to shrink or expand when in use, according to the state of the weather.

If 6 is the last figure upon the strap, it is exactly 26 in. from the end, including the lead, and is the side of the square. The next figure is 7, and so on. The cross-stroke indicates half-inches, and quarter-inches are indicated by the dot. The pole used for taking the height is 14 ft. long, and is marked in feet and half-feet. The lowest mark is at 6 ft., at which height the trees are mostly girthed. Thus by an expeditious and simple process the contents of the first 12 ft. of the trunk are found. Though the use of the slide-rule is recommended for casting up the contents of a tree, yet in extensive practice it is seldom used. Having the length of the section (or whole tree) as indicated by the pole, and the side of the square as shown by the girth, the relative contents soon become so familiar that no casting up is required. In marking the strap it is advantageous to mark one side with white paint for measuring peeled timber, when no allowance is made for the bark; thus the side of the square of a tree 3 ft. in girth is 9 in. The other side may be marked with red paint, allowing for bark at the rate of 1 in. to the foot in girth.

Fallen Timber

G = ¼-girth of tree at middle in feet.
g = " " one end in feet.
g_1 = " " other end in feet.
L = length of log in feet.
c = cubic contents of log in feet.

$$c = L \times [(G + g + g_1) \div 3]^2$$

Allowance should be made for bark by deducting from each quarter-girth. The allowance varies from ½ in. in trees with thin bark to 2 in. in those with thick bark.

G is called the "quarter-girth." It gives a mean between the actual contents and what the tree will square.

No part of a tree is considered timber unless it measures 24 in. in circumference (6 in. quarter-girth).

Valuing Timber

In London the sectional area of square timber is measured by means of the Customs or Queen's callipers; but in Dublin, Glasgow, and other home and American ports by string measurement—that is, by girthing the centre of the balk with a piece of string, and squaring one-fourth of the length of the string. This plan can only be applied with accuracy to square timber; but in string-measuring round timber, the trade custom is the same as if it were square, the log being girthed at two or three points, and one-fourth of its mean girth, less three times the average thickness of the bark, squared for the sectional area.

For finding the true content of a round log stripped of bark, one-fifth of its mean circumference squared, multiplied by twice its length, gives within ½ percent of the correct figure.

Square timber is sold in London by the load of 50 cubic feet, and in some parts by the ton of 40 cubic feet, or by the 50-ft. run at a certain standard percentage over 12 in. square, according to its quality.

Horsepower

The standard of comparison of all power is a "horsepower," which is invariably and universally taken as 33,000 lb. raised 1 ft. high in a minute. This was fixed by Watt from the performance of a London dray-horse, which raised a weight of 150 lb. by a rope passing over a pulley at the rate of 2½ miles an hour, or 220 ft. per minute =33,000 ft. lbs. Good horses will do this for three hours, but for continuous work of eight hours will seldom do more than 23,400 ft. lbs.

SLOPES OF EXCAVATIONS AND EMBANKMENTS

Heights at which different soils will retain a vertical face in excavations for a short time without falling in:

Clean dry sand and gravel	1 ft.
Moist sand and ordinary surface mould	1 ft. to 3 ft.
Loamy soil, well drained	5 " 10 ft.
Ordinary clay	9 " 12 ft.

Chalk and rock will stand perpendicular, or with a slope of about ¼ base to 1 height. In roads it is better to make the sides of cuttings (especially on the south side) with greater slope than they will stand at, to admit sunlight. Earth in embankments should be laid in horizontal courses not more than 4 ft. thick. In high embankments they should be rather concave, to avoid slipping.

Wind Power

V = velocity of wind in fee per second.

P = pressure in lbs. per square foot.

$$P = 0.002288\ V^2$$

$$\text{Horsepower} = A\ V^3 \div 1{,}080{,}000$$

where A = area of sails of windmill in square feet.

The Velocity and Force of Wind

Miles per hour	Fee per second	Force in lb. per sq. ft.	Description
1	1.47	.005	Hardly perceptible
2	2.93	.020	Just
3	4.40	.044	"
4	5.87	0.790	Gentle breeze
5	7.33	0.123	"
10	14.67	0.492	Pleasant

The Velocity and Force of Wind – *Continued*

Miles per hour	Fee per second	Force in lb. per sq. ft.	Description
15	22.0	1.107	Pleasant
20	29.3	1.968	Brisk gale
25	36.6	3.075	"
30	44.0	4.428	High wind
35	51.3	6.027	"
40	58.6	7.872	Very high wind
45	66.0	9.963	"
50	73.3	12.300	Storm
60	88.0	17.712	Great storm
70	102.7	24.108	"
80	117.3	31.488	Hurricane
100	146.6	49.200	Hurricane that tears up trees, etc.

Water Data and Water Power

1 cubic ft. of water = 62.425 lb. = .557 cwt. = .028 ton.
1 cubic in. " = .03612 lb.
1 gallon " = 10 lb. = .16 cubic ft.
1 cubic ft. " = 6.24 gal. = 6¼ gal. (say).
1 cwt. " = 1.8 cubic ft. = 11.2 gal.
1 ton " = 35.9 cubic ft. = 224 gal.
1 cubic ft. of sea water = 64.11 lb. = 1.027 weight of fresh water
1 in. per acre = 101.28 tons = 22,622.52 gal.
P = pressure in lb. per square inch = .4335 lb. per foot in depth.
H = head of water in feet.
V = theoretical velocity in feet per second.
$P = H \times .4335$; $H = P \times 2.307$.
$V = 8.025 \sqrt{H}$; H 62.4 = pressure per square foot.

Theoretical Horsepower of Water

Q = quantity of water in cubic feet per minute.
H = head of water from tail race in feet.
P = theoretical horsepower.
62.5 = weight of cubic foot of water in lb.

$$P = (Q \times 62.5 \times H) \div 33{,}000$$
$$= .001892\ QH$$

Water

	Fresh	Salt
Greatest density at	40° Fahr.	freezing point.
1 cubic foot at 40° weighs	64.425 lb.	64 lb.
1 cubic inch at 40° weighs	.036126 lb.	.037037 lb.
1 cubic foot at 40° equals	6.242 gal.	6.2 gal
1 gal. weighs	10 lb.	10.3 lb.
1 ton equals	35.943 cubic ft.	35 cubic ft.
1 ton contains	224 gal.	217 gal.
Freezes at	32° Fahr.	27° Fahr.

Loads of Carts and Wagons

Ordinary cart takes 1¾ cubic yd.	=	2½	tons	earth.
Dobbin cart takes ¾ cubic yd.	=	1	ton	"
Earth wagon takes 2 cubic yd.	=	3¼	tons	"
Wheelbarrow (navvy) takes .1 cubic yd.	=	3	cwt.	"
Wheelbarrow (ordinary) takes .05 cubic yd.	=	1½	"	"

Acres

Statute or Imperial acre	=	4,840	sq. yds.
Cheshire and Staffs. Acre	=	10,240	"
Cornwall acre	=	5,760	"
Cunningham acre	=	6,250	"
Devon and Somerset acre	=	4,000	"
Wilts and Dorset acre	=	3,630	"
Northumberland and Durham acre	=	5,926.58	"
Scottish (standard) acre	=	6,104.128	"
Irish (plantation) acre	=	7,840	"
French "hectare"	=	11,960.3326	"
" "are"	=	119.6033	"

Superficial Measure

144 square in.	=	1 square ft.
9 square ft.	=	1 square yd.
30¼ square yds.	=	1 square rod, pole, or perch.

"Yards square" and "square yards" are not the same. Thus, 100 square yards are only about the forty-eighth part of an acre, whereas 100 yards square would be nearly 2¼ acres.

40 square poles (1,210 square yds.)	= 1 rood
4 square roods (4,840 square yds. or 160 square poles)	= 1 acre
640 acres	= 1 sq. mi.

Note—The chain used for measuring land is 4 poles or 22 yds. long, and consists of 100 links, each link being 22/100 yds., or 7-92 in. long. 10,000 square links = a square chain; 25,000 square links = a square rood; 100,000 square links or 10 square chains = 1 acre.

Dry or Corn Measure

Quart	=	2 pints	Strike	=	2 bushels
Pottle	=	2 quarts	Coomb	=	4 "
Gallon	=	4 "	Quarter	=	8 "
Peck	=	2 gallons	Load	=	5 quarters
Bushel	=	4 pecks	Last	=	10 "

Hay and Straw Weight

36 lb. avoirdupois of straw			=	1 truss.
56 "	"	old hay	=	1 "
60 "	"	new hay	=	1 "
36 trusses			=	1 load.

Hay is called old after the commencement of September, when it has had time to settle and get thoroughly dry. A load of old hay should weigh 18 cwt., a load of new hay 19 cwt. 32 lb. A load of straw weighs 11 cwt. 64 lb.

The weight of hay per cubic yard in the stack depends on the nature of the hay, its age, the size of the stack, and the part of the stack taken. It varies from 112 lb. to 300 lb. per cubic yard; 196 lb. is an average adopted in the North, but in the South 224 lb. to the cubic yard is considered a good average.

For different conditions of hay and stacks the number of cubic yards to a ton will approximately vary as follows:

*Condition of stack	Square stacks cubic yards	Round stacks cubic yards
If not well settled	12	13
If fairly well settled	10	11
If very compact	8	9

*McConnell's "Agricultural Note Book," Seventh Edition.

In estimating the weight of hay in a stack it is usual to multiply the length of the stack by its breadth and multiply the result by its height, all in feet; divide the total by 27, which will give the number of cubic yards; divide the number of cubic yards by 8, 10, or 12, according to the condition of the stack, as per above table, and the result will be the weight in tons. In measuring the height, deduct two-thirds of the number of feet from the eaves to the top. For example, a stack 20 ft. long and 10 ft. broad thus multiplied is 200 ft.; say, the height to the eaves 10 ft., from the eaves to the top 6 ft.—two-thirds of the last named figure is 4 ft., leaving 2 ft. to be added to the 10 = 12, multiply 200 by 12 = 2,400; then divide 2,400 by 27, which gives nearly 90 cubic yds., and 90 divided by 12 (12 cubic yds. = 1 ton, as per above table) =7½ tons.

Wool Weight

7 lb.	make	1 clove (cl.)
14 lb.	"	1 stone (st.)
2 stones	"	1 tod (td.)
6½ tods	"	1 wey (wy.)
2 weys	"	1 sack (sk.)
12 sacks	"	1 last (la.)

Liquid Measure

4 gills	=	1 pint	=	34.67	cubic in.	(about)
2 pints	=	1 quart	=	69.33	"	"
4 quarts	=	1 gallon	=	277.25	"	"
1.76 pints	=	1 litre				

Quantities of Various Seeds Required Per Statute Acre

Broom	25 lb.	Hungarian forage grass	28 to 40 lb.
Buckwheat	2 bus.	Kidney vetch	25 to 30 lb.
Burnet	40 lb.	Kohl rabi	4 lb.
Cabbage, drilled	4 to 6 lb.	Linseed	2 bus.
Cabbage, transplanting	1 lb.	Lucerne	20 to 28 lb.
Carrot	8 lb.	Lupin	2 bu.
Chicory	8 lb.	Maize	1 to 1½ bus.
Clover	16 to 20 lb.		
Fenugreek	30 lb.	Mangel-wurzel	8 to 10 lb.
Flax	2 bus.	Mustard	20 lb.

Quantities of Various Seeds Required Per Statute Acre – *Continued*

Furze, for cover	30 lb.	Parsnip	8 lb.
" for fodder	40 to 50 lb.	Peas	2 to 3 bus.
		Potatoes	14 cwt.
Grasses and clovers for–		Rape	6 lb.
1 year's ley	20 lb.	Rye grass	3 bus.
2 " "	24 lb.	Sainfoin, in husk	5 bus.
3 " "	32 lb.	" milled	56 lb.
		Sorghum, drill	15 lb.
Grass seeds for–		" broadcast	26 lb.
Putting green, 8-10 bus.	According to	Spurrey	15 lb.
Golf course, 3-10 bus.	circumstance	Sugar-beet	12 lb.
Permanent pasture	40 lb.	Sunflower	8 lb.
Temporary pasture	25 to 40 lb.	Swede	3 or 4 lb.
Renovating pastures	10 to 20 lb.	Trifolium	24 to 28 lb.

To Estimate the Weight of Cattle

Measure round the animal close behind the shoulder, then along the back from the forepart of the shoulder-blade to the bone at the tail. Multiply the square of the girth by five times the length, both expressed in feet. Divide the product by 21, and the result is the approximate weight of the four quarters in stones of 14 lb. Very fat cattle weigh about one-twentieth more, and lean cattle about one-twentieth less, than the result obtained by the above method. The four quarters are little more than half the weight of the animal when living. The skin weighs about one-eighteenth and the tallow about one-twelfth of the whole. As an example of the method employed, if the girth be 7 ft. and the length 5 ft., multiply the square of 7 or 49 by 5 times the length, or 25. This gives 1,225, which, when divided by 21, shows the approximate weight to be 58½ stones of 14 lb.

Cost of Golf Course Implements

Barrows, navvy	12*s*. to 16*s*. each
" garden	24*s*. " 35*s*. "
Brooms, bamboo	2*s*. "
Carts, single horse	£14 to £18 "
" golf roller	£17 " £20 "
" liquid	£15 "
" water (greenkeeper's)	£7 10*s*. to L9 10*s*. each

Cost of Golf Course Implements – Continued

Chaff cutters	30*s*. to 80*s*. each
Corn bins	24*s*. " 27*s*. "
Cultivators	£3 to £8 "
Drill, broadcast, 12 ft.	70*s*. "
Grindstone, 24-in. with frame	48*s*. "
Harrows, chain (5 ft. × 6 ft.)	35*s*. "
" spike	60*s*. to 90*s*. "
Horseshoes	35*s*. " 55*s*. pair
Machines, mowing (men)	£3 to £10 5*s*. each
" " (horse)	£17 10*s*. to £38 each
" golf course mower	£12 each
Motor golf mowers	£130 to £140 each
Plough, single furrow	£3 10*s*. to £6 "
" double	£5 to £7 "
" subsoil	£3 " £5 "
" turf	£8 " £9 "
Rakes, horse	£10 " £12 "
Rollers, Cambridge	£11 " £17 "
" flat	£8 " £15 "
" golf (horse)	£9 " £18 "
" " (men)	25*s*. " 120*s*. "
" wooden	37*s*. " 60*s*. "
Screens (according to mesh)	20*s*. " 25*s*. "
Seed Sower, the Little Wonder	21*s*. "
Tee mats, coir yarn	12*s*. 6*d*. to 41*s*. each
" cocoanut fibre	5*s*. to 11*s*. "
Sieves, hand	3*s*. 6*d*. to 4*s*. "
Turf beaters	5*s*. "
Water barrow, greenkeeper's	42*s*. to 81*s*. "
Wheelbarrows	21*s*. to 27*s*. 6*d*. "

Smaller Tools

Daisy grubber	1*s*. 6*d*. and 2*s*. each
Forks, digging	3*s*. 6*d*. to 6*s*. "
Edging iron	2*s*. 6*d*. " 4*s*. "
" shears	6*s*. to 8*s*. 6*d*. "
Garden lines	1*s*. 6*d*. to 2*s*. 9*d*. each
" reels	3*s*. each
Gorse hooks	2*s*. 6*d*. each

Smaller Tools – *Continued*

Pickaxe	3*s*. 6*d*. each
Rakes, iron	1*s*. 6*d*. to 4*s*. 6*d*. each
" wood	3*s*. each
Scythes	4*s*. "
Scythe-stones	6*d*. "
Shears, hand	3*s*. 6*d*. each
Shovels	4*s*. and 4*s*. 6*d*. each
Spades	3*s*. 9*d*. to 5*s*. 6*d*. each
Turfing irons	7*s*. to 10*s*. each
Turf pricker (Sutton's)	15*s*. each

The Sutton Lawn Mower

Width of Cutter		£	*s*.	*d*.
8-in.	Can be used by a lady or boy	3	0	0
10-in.	" " "	4	2	6
12-in.	" " lad	5	5	0
14-in.	" " man	6	7	6
16-in.	" " " on an even lawn	7	10	0
18-in.	" " " and a boy	8	10	0
20-in.	" " two men	9	5	0
22-in.	" " "	9	15	0
24-in.	The Sutton Lawn Mower*	10	5	0

* Whippletree for pony or donkey 7*s*. 6d. extra.

Larger machines for Pony or Horsepower. (*See pages 211-212.*)

The Sutton Golf Mower

Specially designed for putting greens. Cutters large, with an extra blade; high driving wheels fitted with ball bearings. The mower may be set to cut very closely. By an ingenious arrangement the machine can be inverted and pushed from one green to another. Runs with remarkable ease and freedom. Price of 19-in. golf mower, easily worked by one man, £7 10*s*. (with removable grass-box). Smaller sizes are 17-in. machines at £6 12*s*. 6*d*., and 15-in. machines at £5 15*s*. 6*d*.

Tables and Decimal Weights and Measures

Accurately compared with the Weights and Measures of England.

French and English Coins

English Coinage.	*Value in France.*
The crown piece	Six francs twenty-five centimes
" half-crown piece	Three francs twelve and a half centimes
" shilling	One franc twenty-five centimes
" sixpence	Sixty-two and a half centimes
" penny	Ten centimes
" halfpenny	Five centimes

French Coinage.	*English Value.* £	*s.*	*d.*
A piece of five francs	0	4	0
" one franc	0	0	9½
" a demi-franc, or fifty centimes	0	0	4¾
" two sous, one decime, or ten centimes	0	0	1
" one sou, or five centimes	0	0	0½
A napoleon, or twenty-franc piece	0	16	0

Table of Wages

	£	*s.*	*d.*	£	*s.*	*d.*	£	*s.*	*d.*
Per day (6 to week)	0	0	10	0	1	0	0	1	2
Per week	0	5	0	0	6	0	0	7	0
Per annum	13	0	0	15	12	0	18	4	0
Per day (6 to week)	0	2	0	0	2	2	0	2	4
Per week	0	12	0	0	13	0	0	14	0
Per annum	31	4	0	33	16	0	36	8	0
Per day (6 to week)	0	3	2	0	3	4	0	3	6
Per week	0	19	0	1	0	0	1	1	0
Per annum	49	8	0	52	0	0	54	12	0

Table of Wages – *Continued*

	£	s.	d.	£	s.	d.	£	s.	d.
Per day (6 to week)	0	1	4	0	1	6	0	1	8
Per week	0	8	0	0	9	0	0	10	0
Per annum	20	16	0	23	8	0	26	0	0
Per day (6 to week)	0	2	6	0	2	8	0	2	10
Per week	0	15	0	0	16	0	0	17	0
Per annum	39	0	0	41	12	0	44	4	0
Per day (6 to week)	0	3	8	0	3	10	0	4	0
Per week	1	2	0	1	3	0	1	4	0
Per annum	57	4	0	59	16	0	62	8	0

Measures of Length

	English Inches.	Miles.	Furlongs.	Yards.	Feet.	Inches.
Millimetre	.03937	–	–	–	–	–
Centimetre	.39371	–	–	–	–	–
Decimetre	3.93710	–	–	–	–	–
Metre	39.37100	–	–	–	–	–
Decametre	393.71000	0	0	10	2	9
Hectometre	3937.10000	0	0	109	1	1
Kilometre	39371.00000	0	4	213	1	10.2
Myriametre	393710.00000	6	1	156	0	6

		Metres.	Millim.
1 mile (8 furlongs) equivalent to		1609	314
1 furlong (40 poles)	”	201	165
1 pole, perch (5½ yards)	”	5	029
1 fathom (2 yards)	”	1	828
1 yard (3 feet)	”	0	914
1 foot (12 inches)	”	0	304
1 inch	”	0	025½
French ell (1½ yard)	”	1	371
French ell (1¼ yard)	”	1	142½
1 quarter (4 nails)	”	0	228
1 nail (2¼ inches)	”	0	057

The terms used in the metrical system are five principal, with four to express increase and three to express decrease.

The five principal are: For long and square measure, the metre; for land measure, the are; for wood, the stere; for measures of capacity, the litre; and the gramme for weights.

The four terms which express increases are:

Deca, which signifies		tenfold.
Hecto	"	one hundredfold.
Kilo	"	one thousandfold.
Myria	"	one thousandfold.

The three terms which express decreases are:

Deci, which signifies the		tenth part.
Centi	"	hundredth part.
Milli	"	thousandth part.

The names of all weights and measures are formed by a union of one of these principal terms with one of increase or decrease. Kilogramme, for example, is kilo (1,000 fold) and gramme, and signifies 1,000 grammes. Decimetre is deci (the tenth part) and metre, and signifies the tenth part of a metre. Decametre is deca (tenfold) and metre, and signifies 10 metres.

Capacity

	Cubic Inches.	Tuns.	Hhds.	Wine Gals.	Pints.
Millilitre	.06102	—	—	—	—
Centilitre	.61028	—	—	—	—
Decilitre	6.10280	—	—	—	—
Litre	61.02800	—	—	—	2.1133
Decalitre	610.28000	—	—	—	5.1152
Hectolitre	6102.80000	—	—	26.491	—
Kilolitre	62018.00000	1	—	12.19	—
Myrialitre	610280.00000	10	1	58.9	—

Dry Measures. Grain

	Litres.	Centilit.
1 quarter (8 bushels)	290	78
1 bushel (4 pecks)	36	34
1 peck (2 gallons)	9	08
1 gallon (2 pottles)	4	54
1 pottle (2 quarts)	2	27
1 quart (2 pints)	1	13½
1 pint	—	56¾

Measures of Weight

	Grains	Pounds	Ounces	Drams
Milligramme	.0154	—	—	—
Centigramme	.1544	—	—	—
Decigramme	1.5444	—	—	—
Gramme	15.4440	—	—	—
Decagramme	154.4402	—	—	5.65
Hectogramme	1544.4023	—	3	8.5
Kilogramme	15444.0234	2	3	5
Myriagramme	154440.2344	22	1	2

The French pound of 16 ozs. is equal to 400 grammes; 100 lb. to 49 kilogrammes. The demi-kilogramme (500 grammes) replaces the old pound, and is convenient on that account in usual transactions; it is equal to 1 lb. 3 gros old French weight.

Avoirdupois Weight

	Grammes.	Centigr.
1 ton (20 quintals) equivalent to	1015649	20
1 quintal (112 pounds)	50782	46
1 pound (lb. 16 ounces)	453	41
1 ounce (oz. 16 drams)	28	33
1 dram	1	77

Troy Weight

1 pound (12 ounces)	373	09
1 ounce (oz. 20 pennyweights)	31	09
1 pennyweight (dwt. 24 grains)	1	55

A Table Reducing French Francs and Centimes to their Value in English Pounds, Shillings, and Pence

Cts.	£	*s.*	*d.*	*Cts.*	£	*s.*	*d.*	*Fr.*	£	*s.*	*d.*	*Fr.*	£	*s.*	*d.*
5	0	0	0½	75	0	0	7	9	0	7	2	50	2	0	0
10	0	0	1	80	0	0	7½	10	0	8	0	60	2	8	0
15	0	0	1½	85	0	0	8	11	0	8	9½	70	2	16	0
20	0	0	2	90	0	0	8½	12	0	9	7	80	3	4	0
25	0	0	2¼	95	0	0	9	13	0	10	4½	90	3	12	0
30	0	0	2¾	*Fr.*				14	0	11	2	100	4	0	0
35	0	0	3¼	1	0	0	9½	15	0	12	0	200	8	0	0
40	0	0	3¾	2	0	1	7	16	0	12	9½	300	12	0	0
45	0	0	4¼	3	0	2	4½	17	0	13	7	400	16	0	0
50	0	0	4¾	4	0	3	2	18	0	14	4½	500	20	0	0
55	0	0	5¼	5	0	4	0	19	0	15	2	750	30	0	0
60	0	0	5¾	6	0	4	9½	20	0	16	0	1,000	40	0	0
65	0	0	6¼	7	0	5	7	30	1	4	0	5,000	200	0	0
70	0	0	6¾	8	0	6	4½	40	1	12	0	10,000	400	0	0

The amounts under one franc in value are calculated within 1/8th of a penny.

A Table Reducing English Money to its Value in Francs and Centimes

d.	*f.*	*c.*	*s.*	*f.*	*c.*	*L*	*f.*	*c.*	*L*	*f.*	*c.*
1	0	10½	6	7	50	3	70	0	20	500	0
2	0	21	7	8	75	4	100	0	30	750	0
3	0	31½	8	10	0	5	125	0	40	1,000	0
4	0	42	9	11	25	6	150	0	50	1,250	0
5	0	52½	10	12	50	7	175	0	60	1,500	0
6	0	63	11	13	75	8	200	0	70	1,750	0
7	0	73½	12	15	0	9	225	0	80	2,000	0
8	0	84	13	16	25	10	250	0	90	2,250	0
9	0	94½	14	17	50	11	275	0	100	2,500	0
10	1	5	15	18	75	12	300	0	200	5,000	0
11	1	15	16	20	0	13	325	0	300	7,500	0

	F.	C.
Note—English Sovereign at the par of Exchange	25	21
" Crown " "	6	30½
" Shilling " "	1	26

Index

M

N – O

P

Q – R

S

T

U – V

W

X – Z

CPSIA information can be obtained
at www.ICGtesting.com
Printed in the USA
LVHW011934230821
695886LV00005B/661

9 781732 113770